Author: GREGORY McNAMEE
Book Designer: KRIS SOTELO
Photography Editor: JEFF KIDA
Book Editor: BETH DEVENY
Copy Editor: EVELYN HOWELL
Map and Illustrations: KEVIN KIBSEY

Library of Congress Control Number: 2007924959
ISBN: 978-1-932082-78-4
First Printing: 2007. Second Printing: 2008. Third Printing: 2011.
Printed in Singapore.

Published by the Book Division of *Arizona Highways* magazine,
a monthly publication of the Arizona Department of Transportation,
2039 West Lewis Avenue, Phoenix, Arizona 85009.
Telephone: (602) 712-2200
Website: www.arizonahighways.com

Publisher: WIN HOLDEN
Editor: ROBERT STIEVE
Senior Editor/Books: RANDY SUMMERLIN
Creative Director: BARBARA GLYNN DENNEY
Photography Editor: JEFF KIDA
Production Director: MICHAEL BIANCHI
Production Assistants: ANNETTE PHARES, DIANA BENZEL-RICE

COVER: A small canyon winds through the fluted sandstone of
Vermilion Cliffs National Monument. DAVID ELMS JR.

INSETS TOP TO BOTTOM: The weathered stones of Wupatki National Monument bask in the
warm light after a summer thunderstorm. GEORGE H.H. HUEY

Monsoon clouds tower over a saguaro grove in Saguaro National Park. JACK DYKINGA

The Grand Canyon, seen in this upstream view from Toroweap, is an ever-changing play
of water, stone, and light. TOM DANIELSEN

PREVIOUS PAGE: A balanced boulder greets the sky along the Echo Park Trail, Chiricahua
National Monument. GEORGE STOCKING

OPPOSITE: A sandstone hoodoo gleams mysteriously at twilight, White Pocket, Vermilion
Cliffs National Monument. CLAIRE CURRAN

CONTENTS PAGE: With more than 150 rooms, Keet Seel cliff dwelling, in Navajo National
Monument, was an important center of Ancestral Puebloan life. GEORGE H.H. HUEY

MONUMENTAL
PLACES

national parks and monuments in the grand canyon state

by Gregory McNamee
Images by *Arizona Highways* Photographers

UTAH

NEVADA

COLORADO PLATEAU

COLORADO

Colorado River

Lake Powell

Vermilion Cliffs
National Monument

Fredonia

Page

Navajo National
Monument

Pipe Spring
National Monument

89A

89

Kayenta

Grand Canyon-Parashant
National Monument

Colorado River

GRAND CANYON

160

Canyon de Chelly
National Monument

Grand Canyon
National Park

Lake Mead

Chinle

191

Lake Mohave

Wupatki National
Monument

Hubbell Trading Post
National Historic Site

Ganado

Kingman

40

89

FLAGSTAFF

Sunset Crater Volcano
National Monument

Petrified Forest
National Park

Walnut Canyon
National Monument

ARIZONA

40

Holbrook

CALIFORNIA

Tuzigoot National
Monument

Little Colorado River

Cottonwood

260

Montezuma Castle
National Monument

MOGOLLON RIM

Lake Havasu

Camp Verde

Bill Williams River

Agua Fria
National Monument

Theodore Roosevelt
Lake

Salt River

Hassayampa River

Agua Fria River

17

Verde River

Tonto National
Monument

88

Colorado River

10

PHOENIX

Salt River

Globe

San Carlos
Reservoir

SONORAN

Mesa

60

10

Gila River

Sonoran Desert
National Monument

Casa Grande Ruins
National Monument

Yuma

DESERT

8

Gila River

85

Casa Grande

Gila River

Santa Cruz River

USA
MEXICO

Ajo

Saguaro
National Park
(West Unit)

Ironwood Forest
National Monument

Fort Bowie National
Historic Site

TUCSON

Willcox

Organ Pipe Cactus
National Monument

Saguaro
National Park
(East Unit)

186

19

Chiricahua National
Monument

Tumacácori National
Historical Park

90

San Pedro River

GULF

USA
MEXICO

Sierra Vista

OF

Nogales

Coronado National
Memorial

CALIFORNIA

MEXICO

NEW MEXICO

Artist: KEVIN KIBSEY

contents

introduction

arizona's national treasures

There is a place where blue-green water cascades over waterfalls a dozen stories high, where ferns and agaves grow side by side, where walls of stone drop thousands of feet and condors soar overhead.

There is a place where the wind whistles across the face of sweeping sandstone cliffs. Within them the long-abandoned homes of ancient peoples lie silent, keeping age-old secrets.

There is a place where a great maze of water-carved boulders rises along the spines of tall mountains. There indigenous warriors held newcomers at bay for generations, and the earth trembled.

There is a place where giant cacti stand tall against a brilliant blue sky, sheltering dozens of plant and animal species, their odd forms so closely resembling humans that the people consider them to be kin in their desert homeland.

All these places—respectively, Grand Canyon, Canyon de Chelly, the Chiricahua Mountains, and Saguaro National Park—lie within the borders of Arizona, a state that, as newcomers will discover and even old-timers find it surprising to learn, contains broadly diverse environments and ecosystems. Let us take an eagle's eye tour, beginning on the straight-edge northern line that finds Arizona greeting Utah and Nevada at its western terminus and Utah, New Mexico, and Colorado at its eastern one. As we follow red sandstone escarpments, slot canyons, intermittent streams, and spire-strewn valleys eastward, we mark the contours of the high Colorado Plateau. From there, we track straight south across forested mountain ranges, yucca-studded cliffs, and grassy valleys, the highlands where many of Arizona's rivers are born. We turn west in wild mountains, stair-stepping through grasslands, cactus forests, sand dunes, and lava chaos. Then we turn north again, following the great, muddy Colorado River.

Our survey completed, we have described the borders of 113,909 square miles of some of the most varied landscapes on the planet. And within those landscapes lie Arizona's incomparable national parks and monuments, where all these majestic, transformative sights can be seen.

Arizona is host to 25 such parks and monuments, along with historic sites—far more than any other single state, a generous share of the 390 national parks, monuments, and historic sites that grace our country. Although it has long borne the proud sobriquet "Grand Canyon State," Arizona saw the seeds of its contributions to the national system planted well before statehood, and not at its most famous scenic destination. Rather, the Casa Grande Ruins, lying between Phoenix and Tucson, earned the earliest federal designation in Arizona and the third earliest in the nation (after Hot Springs, Arkansas, and Yellowstone). It was authorized in 1889 and established in 1892 as the Casa Grande Ruin Reservation, then reclassified as a national monument in 1918. The second national monument in Arizona, again predating statehood, was created in 1906 at the Petrified Forest, where the renowned naturalist and conservationist John Muir had spent a season and then got busy petitioning his friend Theodore Roosevelt, then president of the United States, to set it aside for posterity. Roosevelt did Muir more than one better: The same day, he designated Montezuma Castle as a national monument; in 1907, he created Tonto National Monument; and in 1908, he added the Grand Canyon and Tumacácori Mission to the national roster. Grand Canyon graduated to national park status in 1919, Petrified Forest long afterward, in 1962. In the intervening years, all but a handful of Arizona's current parks, monuments, and historic sites had joined the present roster.

Now, a national monument is distinguished from a national park in fairly subjective terms. A monument contains a particular thing that merits preservation, such as the ruins of an ancient Native American structure or a rare or especially significant type of plant, animal, or environment; in Arizona's case, Navajo National Monument and Organ Pipe Cactus National Monument serve as examples, respectively. A national park, conversely, is usually set aside for protection because it is considered to be particularly scenic. A president can create a

national monument, but Congress must sign off on a national park; national parks usually provide more than one point of interest and a range of visitor services, as can be found at the Grand Canyon, while national monuments may not have a permanent ranger station or visitors center, as visitors to our Tuzigoot and Parashant national monuments know. Monuments are often elevated to parks in time, once the extent of their importance is realized. And in this dance of designations, new sites worthy of protection join the roll from time to time, as with the recently established Sonoran Desert National Monument, in the lovely desert country southwest of Phoenix.

All those technicalities aside, Arizona's national parks, monuments, and historic sites share this in common: They rank high among the list of reasons that visitors come to our state, and they are cherished uncommonly well by those who live here, receiving the benefit of what might be called "internal tourism" at all times of year. After the Great Smoky Mountains National Park, Grand Canyon was the second-most-visited park in the nation in

2005. Saguaro National Park receives a steady flow of visitors across the seasons. And, though the winter can be cold and the summer hot in our corner of the world, even Canyon de Chelly, Organ Pipe, and Petrified Forest seldom are without travelers from near and far, no matter what date the calendar shows.

The names ring in an exotic honor roll: Chiricahua, Wupatki, Vermilion Cliffs, Coronado, Montezuma Well, Walnut Canyon, Agua Fria. Arizona's national parks, monuments, and historic sites offer fascinating voyages into the natural and human history of this vast and varied place. We welcome you to share, enjoy, and protect this great heritage.

OPPOSITE: A blue-green pool at Pumpkin Springs, deep in the heart of Grand Canyon National Park, beckons invitingly. JEFF FOOTT/LARRY ULRICH STOCK

ABOVE: A gnarled juniper meets an iron-rich sandstone formation in Vermilion Cliffs National Monument. JACK DYKINGA

At sunset, the Grand Canyon reveals itself layer upon layer in this view from Lipan Point, near the east entrance to the South Rim. GEORGE STOCKING

the
immensity
of time

grand canyon national park

grand canyon national park

this is a world of opposites: night and day, black and white, hot and cold, raw and cooked. At the Grand Canyon, where mountain meets chasm, another opposite comes into play: solid and void. You can feel the void before you ever see it, entering the park through a dense forest of ponderosa pines that suddenly ends in open space and great sweeping vistas as far as your eye can see.

When you do see it, all that vastness can play havoc with your senses.

Some people who come to the Grand Canyon feel strangely insignificant, dwarfed by the sheer, barely fathomable, oversized scale of the place; any place that suddenly gives way to a mile-deep fall, in which the whole of humankind past and present could easily be hidden, can make a single individual feel unaccountably tiny.

Faced with the incomparable grandeur of the Grand Canyon, other people feel exalted, spiritually elevated. Though it is flat, the plateau leading to the Canyon is what one indigenous people called a "mountain lying down," lifted up toward the heavens over endless eons of geology. Mountains in all their forms, even flattish ones, are traditionally associated with deities and spirits, not so much because they are high relative to their surroundings, but because from them you can truly see forever, giving us a larger-than-life feeling that

resembles extrasensory perception. Standing there at the edge of the world, at the lip of what the Navajos call *Tsékooh Hatsoh*, "rock canyon of great space," and the Hopi call *Ongtupka*, "home of the ancestors," I always find my senses sharpening, my eyesight and hearing becoming just a touch more acute. That reaction is most satisfying, particularly as the years conspire to take that sharpness away, though I expect that at least some of it is driven by the vertigo that latches hold of me from time to time, naturally enough in inconvenient moments while negotiating high and steep places such as this.

Then there are those rare souls who seemingly are unmoved by the vastness and depth of the Grand Canyon, such as Marshal Ferdinand Foch, the French commander in chief of the Allied forces in World War I. After the war, he toured the United States and was taken to see the Grand Canyon, where he spent hours gazing into its depths, transfixed. Finally he turned to his American escort and exclaimed, "What a wonderful place to drop one's mother-in-law!"

Having no malign feelings toward my mother-in-law, I prefer to take the good marshal's *bon mot* metaphorically: The Grand Canyon is a wonderful place to let go of yourself, if even for just a moment, and contemplate the immensity of time. Stand at the South Rim and gaze at the vast palisade of rock 10 miles distant, the walls of the

OPPOSITE: The Grand Canyon, seen in this upstream view from Toroweap, at the Canyon's western end, is an ever-changing play of water, stone, and light. TOM DANIELSEN

BELOW LEFT: Dana Butte, in the center distance, looms over the swirling Colorado River within Grand Canyon National Park. JACK DYKINGA

BELOW RIGHT: A storm sweeps across the Grand Canyon in this view from Pima Point, on the South Rim. TOM DANIELSEN

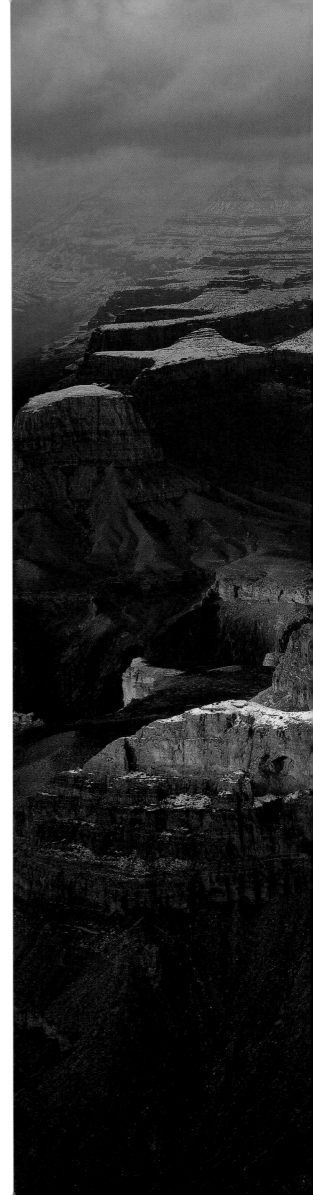

North Rim, and you face some 2 billion years of the Earth's history. The darkest rocks, near the Colorado River far below, were once layers of sand, shale, and limestone pressed and melted into granite by volcanic action. Long ago they lay far under the Earth's surface, as much as 12 miles down, before that great superimposed mass wore down over thousands of millennia.

Let your eye take in the depths of Bright Angel Canyon opposite Grand Canyon Village, and you can see the dark layers of the dark orange Hakatai shale and Cardenas lavas, rocks that are a billion years old and once made up tall mountains of the basin-and-range type, very much like the Sierra Ancha outside Phoenix or the Santa Catalinas above Tucson. Somewhere in all that geological ebb and flow, a big chunk of the record has gone missing, the rocks representing the time from about 250 million to 1.2 billion years ago. The Earth has swallowed them, not only at the Grand Canyon, but also at other points around the globe, yielding the puzzling phenomenon that geologists call the Great Unconformity.

The immensity of time: If the dizzying depths of the Grand Canyon weren't enough to do the job, the thought can make your head spin.

My first trip to the Grand Canyon, in 1975, was in the company of budding geologists, part of a geosciences laboratory class at the University of Arizona. I was newly arrived from Virginia, still a little green, certainly untested. Most of the Westerners among my fellow students were rough-and-ready types; one, who improbably survived the experience to become a well-known archaeologist, accompanied me down the unmaintained Grandview Trail wearing cowboy boots. Another wore beat-up tennis shoes.

That seemed to me then a species of madness, but, as the adage goes, what doesn't kill you makes you stronger. I tested that saying time and again over the years, descending various trails to the river, 26 times in all, always wearing sturdy hiking boots. That got me thinking that I was a pretty durable fellow myself, until I met a fellow who regularly ran from rim to rim to rim, departing at dawn from the South Rim in track shoes and running shorts, showing up at the North Rim at about noon for a bite of lunch, then returning to Grand Canyon Village on the South Rim in time for supper. I admired his stamina, though his talk of having found a vast hidden lake down in Bright Angel Canyon made me think that one too many stray rays of sunlight had pierced his brain.

Still, the Canyon is a place where just about anything can happen. Once, dangling my feet over a ledge on Horseshoe Mesa, still a quarter-mile above the Canyon floor, I was startled out of my skin at the sight of a hand, then another, coming up over the sheer wall. A leathery face followed, burned by the sun, eyes seemingly as yellow as old Sol. "Got any water?" he asked. "Got any food? A cigarette?" On the run from the law, the fellow—who disappeared as swiftly

as he had appeared—had been hiding out in the inner Canyon for months, though he apparently thought nothing of coming up for supplies from time to time.

Once, I happened upon a despondent Englishman who had been at the South Rim for a week but had never seen the Grand Canyon.

That may seem paradoxical, but as it happened, it was winter, when clouds often sock in the landscape for days at a time. After a cup of coffee, I invited him to walk with me to the Powell Memorial, then waved my hand in a sort of presto-change-o motion, whereupon the clouds parted and a great shaft of sunlight broke through, illuminating the gorge for a few brilliant moments. I was as surprised as the English visitor at this bit of good fortune, but I blew on my fingertips and asked, "Did you like how I did that?"

Delusions of grandeur don't come easily at the human-grandeur-deflating Grand Canyon, but big plans have often inspired the people who have made their way here. Below the Powell Memorial, a good way down, stands Bass Camp, where pioneer William Wallace Bass, who arrived at the Canyon in 1883, pretty much single-handedly built a cable car to cross the river, planning for crowds of miners and tourists who, back then, failed to show up in sufficient numbers. Bass was undaunted, and he made a fine contraption. "The cable affords a fair crossing of the river at this point, and with a man on top of the car to operate the windlass, a horse can be carried across, if he is a tractable animal," wrote Canyon explorer Claude Birdseye, whose happy name suited the vistas he took in.

Bass's son William, a chronicler of the Canyon, grew up at Bass Camp. "I was born in Williams, Arizona, July 26, 1900," he recalled, "only missing being born at Bass Camp by one week, as it was necessary for my mother to be taken to the nearest hospital and doctor. As soon as she could travel again, I was back at home on the Rim; so I say I was practically the first white child born on the Rim of the Grand Canyon. I also feel that I inherited the Grand Canyon. . . . I was born with its magical spell in my veins. It was an important part of my parents' lives. It was my first impression of the world, my first realization of things about me."

That's quite an impression, and it is one that Bass never tired of. I have never tired of the Grand Canyon, either: Constantly changing, though seemingly eternal, it's one of those places that can never quite be pegged in memory outside of a general sense of vastness. Some 277 miles long by 5 to 18 miles wide, the national park portion of the Grand Canyon takes in whole worlds, and ten lifetimes would not be sufficient to explore it.

It is almost a cliché to call it a place of magic, but the Canyon has exercised a special power ever since humans came to know it. Havasupai elder Earl Paya tells a tale of how the ancestral mother of his people warned her two sons that the area around the famed blue-green waterfalls of Supai was dangerous. "It's a bad place to go because it kills people," she said. "The rocks go back and forth, coming together and crushing the people who go there." The boys, who wanted to harvest some reeds to use in hunting, were

OPPOSITE: Of time and the river flowing: The Colorado River flows through Lava Falls, in the western end of Grand Canyon National Park. TOM DANIELSEN

TOP: At Elves Chasm, a fittingly named wonderland deep within the Grand Canyon, waterfalls cascade over rock carpeted with ferns and monkeyflowers. JACK DKYINGA

BOTTOM: Shadows fill the canyons of the North Rim of the Grand Canyon, with a view from Point Imperial to Mount Hayden, in the foreground. WILLARD CLAY

undaunted and climbed up to the place called Hualapai Hilltop to watch the rocks clang into each other whenever some unsuspecting person or animal passed between them. One of the boys said, "Let's go down there. But we should cut a piece of log and put it across our shoulders. When the rocks go apart we can run down, grab some plants, and come back. When the rocks come together again, the log will keep it open." That's just how it happened, which is why the Havasupai people call Havasu Canyon *Wii Ggaaba*, "where the rocks come together." Concluding his story, Mr. Paya ventured the opinion that the boys should have used a bigger log and carved out a bigger canyon.

Most of us would agree that the Grand Canyon is big enough, but of course it is always changing, always growing, getting bigger a few centimeters here, a meter there, as rain falls and boulders fall. Cross over to one of my favorite places, Point Imperial on the North Rim, and allow your eye to follow the stream that falls just to the south. This is Nankoweap Creek, whose lovely name comes from a Paiute phrase meaning something like "place that echoes." It certainly does, and far down in the Canyon the air rings with the inviting clatter of water on rock. Balm for a desert rat's soul, that sound speaks to an important fact of North Rim topography: About 1,800 feet taller than the South Rim at this point, the North Rim sees much more snowfall in winter and consequently sheds more water. It has been this way for eons, with endless streams of water flowing north to south, dropping from rim to river through dozens of winding chasms. The result is that the forces of erosion have been at work more forcefully here than they have on the other side of the Colorado River. Look across to the Palisades of the Desert to the east, and you'll see that it's a comparatively straight drop to the river, whereas from the vantage of Point Imperial, miles of deep-cut, churned-up landscape lie between river and rim, all carved out by roiling, freezing, flowing water over millions of years.

For those who prize pleasant backcountry roads, the winding lane that leads from State Route 67 to Point Imperial is one of the greatest pleasures of the national park. It is not the highest road in the United States, but it is certainly high enough, ending one of its extensions at the Grand Canyon's highest point. Plenty of our

ABOVE: A thirsty mule deer pauses to take a drink of water from the Colorado River. DUGALD BREMNER

RIGHT: An ancient Ancestral Puebloan granary affords a commanding view of Marble Canyon, at the eastern end of Grand Canyon National Park. JACK DYKINGA

TOP: Desert mariposa lily and claretcup cactus lend beautiful hues to the Granite Gorge, Grand Canyon National Park. LARRY ULRICH

MIDDLE: Aspens burst forth in summer greenery at the appropriately named Greenland Lake, on the North Rim. LARRY ULRICH

BOTTOM: A raven claims a corner of the Grand Canyon as his very own. DUGALD BREMNER

nation's roads are lonelier, too, but the well-maintained, paved route to Point Imperial, and to Cape Royal some 15 miles beyond, sees little traffic compared to most other Grand Canyon venues; the remote North Rim sees just one visitor for every ten the South Rim draws, and the Point Imperial–Cape Royal Road sees only a small number of the travelers who come to the North Rim.

Call me antisocial, but though I love the society of humankind in the abstract, when it comes to practical terms, a little breathing space is always best. That's one reason that I like to come to the Canyon in winter, when piercing cold settles in the high country and the Grand Canyon takes on an entirely different aspect from that of the usual postcards. The crowds of sightseers disappear with the changing of the leaves, and by the first snowfall, the place is almost deserted. The snow keeps coming and coming, until it seals off the Canyon from the rest of the world—a solitude that Marguerite Henry ably captures in her beloved children's book *Brighty of the Grand Canyon*, celebrating the adventures of a little burro back in the days when the place was the province of only prospectors, hunters, a few pioneer farmers, and the odd outlaw, such as the fellow I met all those years later down on Horseshoe Mesa.

The North Rim is snowier still, the highest point on the Colorado Plateau, which in turn is the highest major plateau in the world, after Tibet. From the vantage point of a traveler cruising along its smooth grade, the climb to the Kaibab Plateau from the rolling tablelands to the north and east is easy enough. But walk or bicycle up that same road, or have a good look at it from, say, the outskirts of the little Arizona town of Fredonia an hour to the north, and you will see that the plateau is an island of whitish rock that rises above the sandy desert of the Arizona Strip like an imposing iceberg from a vermilion sea.

Driving this road over the years and decades, I have pondered the things that make this place so different from the surrounding desert: the geographical isolation that has enabled unique animal populations such as the Kaibab squirrel to develop here and nowhere else, and that has made the plateau so inviting to wildlife of all kinds; the difficult terrain, crisscrossed by tall escarpments and deep-cut valleys, that harbors all kinds of surprises, from small lakes to winding caves; and the geological treasures that the Kaibab Plateau shelters—all in addition, of course, to the Grand Canyon itself.

The Mormon pioneers who came to this place in the mid-19th century called the plateau Buckskin Mountain, after the abundant herds

of deer that, then as now, roamed the highlands above the Colorado River. And highlands they are: At Point Imperial, which stands at 8,803 feet above sea level, the Colorado River lies exactly 6,600 feet below. It's a dizzying drop to that strand of shimmering water, which can be seen from many points along the North Rim but just as often hides itself away behind the great rock reefs that bear such sonorous names as King Arthur Castle and Sagittarius Ridge.

Still more dazzling is the view, for from Point Imperial the vista stretches for more than a hundred miles. The panorama includes a sweeping view of the Vermilion Cliffs and Navajo Mountain to the north, and the pastel-hued Painted Desert and the confluence of the Little Colorado River with the Colorado to the east. Here, below the tall, dusty-rose cliffs called the Palisades of the Desert, the narrow walls of Marble Canyon widen into the broad expanse of what is now the Grand Canyon proper. It is just this view that, perhaps better than any other to be found on either rim, shows why the Grand Canyon deserves its exalted name.

The road continues on to Greenland Lake, a smallish pond formed by a natural spring, that rarest of jewels on the arid plateau. "Greenland" may have reminded the Mormon pioneers, many of Scandinavian descent, of the ice-clad Atlantic island, but it seems more likely that the area was so called just because its ponderosa pine and juniper forests were verdant, certainly in contrast to the arid canyons that tumble down from its sides. But then, today's maps call this place the Walhalla Plateau, a name that at first blush seems a little out of place. Why, after all, name a forest in Arizona after the legendary mountain fortress where dead Viking heroes went to their eternal reward?

The answer lies in a curious footnote to Grand Canyon history. If you look at a map of the Canyon as a whole, you will see many names that speak to local facts: Cardenas Butte, for instance, which commemorates the first European to have visited the area; Chuar Creek, which commemorates a Kaibab Indian who helped guide the American explorer John Wesley Powell; Horseshoe Mesa, which fittingly describes a U-shaped rise below the South Rim. But many other place names are exotic: the cluster of names that come from the tales of King Arthur, the "temples" and "shrines" named after Hindu, Egyptian, and Greek deities—and, here at the eastern end of the Grand Canyon, names taken from ancient Scandinavian tales honoring the likes of Thor, Wotan, and Freya.

Press onward a couple of miles beyond Greenland Lake, and we come to 8,429-foot

ABOVE: Deep within Granite Gorge, in the heart of Grand Canyon, rowers take their dory down a momentarily gentle Colorado River. LARRY ULRICH

Roosevelt Point, named to honor President Theodore Roosevelt, who designated the Grand Canyon a national monument nearly a century ago. Strangely, for so central a figure in Grand Canyon history, Roosevelt did not receive this honor until 1996, and the name is the most recent addition to the national park's map.

A place of gods and heroes, then; a place of magic, and without a bad seat in the house, or an uninspiring view from any overlook. Wherever you arrive in the Grand Canyon, you will have come a long way. To this distance let us add the dimension of time, millions of years' worth of rainfall, wind, and the movement of the earth in carving out the magnificent landscapes that lie before us. It makes for an incomparable journey.

The Grand Canyon inspires awe, reverence, tranquility, and even terror, depending on the view of its beholder. I promise you this: Wherever you come from, wherever you arrive here, wherever you catch your first glimpse of the void, what you have seen in this lofty place will never leave you.

Location

South Rim: Approximately 230 miles north of Phoenix. From Phoenix, take Interstate 17 north to Flagstaff, then merge onto Interstate 40 west toward Williams, approximately 30 miles. At Exit 165, take State Route 64 north for approximately 60 miles to Grand Canyon Village.

North Rim: In northern Coconino County, approximately 320 miles north of Phoenix. From Phoenix, take I-17 north to Flagstaff. At Exit 340A, follow I-40 east approximately 5.5 miles to the exit for Page and the Grand Canyon (U.S. Route 89). Merge onto U.S. 89 and follow it north approximately 105 miles to the U.S. Alternate Route 89 turnoff at Bitter Springs. Follow U.S. 89A via Lee's Ferry approximately 55 miles to Jacob Lake. Turn south on State Route 67 (North Rim Parkway) and follow it approximately 31 miles to the Grand Canyon National Park North Rim entrance station.

Activities

South Rim: Hiking, horse and mule riding, camping, bicycling. The South Rim is open year-round, though winter weather may be severe.

North Rim: Hiking, camping, bicycling. The North Rim of Grand Canyon National Park is open from mid-May to mid-October, when snow usually closes the highway. Daytime use of the park is permitted off-season, though no services are available.

On both the North and South rims, the National Park Service offers a series of instructional and recreational programs—including geology talks, guided walks and hikes, and stargazing sessions—throughout the season.

For more information

Grand Canyon National Park
P.O. Box 129
Grand Canyon, AZ 86023
(928) 638-7888
www.nps.gov/grca

Pipe Spring National Monument

Water is rare in the desert, rarer still in the high-desert country called the Arizona Strip, which lies separated from the rest of the state by the imposing barrier of the Grand Canyon and its tributaries. Thus it was that when Mormon pioneers entered the area in the 1860s, driving church-owned herds to winter pasturage, they were overjoyed to discover a steady source of water at a place they called Pipe Spring—so called, it appears, because of a shooting contest that involved a rifle, considerable distance, and a pioneer's clay pipe, which did not survive the ordeal.

The Mormons were far from the first people to enjoy the grassy, cottonwood-shaded spring. For generations, it had figured in the secular and sacred geography of the Paiute Indians, who lived on the Kaibab Plateau, the "mountain lying down." Even before then, Ancestral Puebloan people had established lowland gardens at the spring, which provided perennial nourishment for crops of corn, beans, chiles, and other staple foods.

In 1870, an entrepreneur and rancher named A.P. Winsor settled at the spring, charged by Mormon patriarch Brigham Young with maintaining the herd of cattle. Winsor promptly set about building the fortress, locally called "Winsor Castle." Smallish but quite secure, the sandstone compound may not have impressed the crowned heads of England, but it became an important and much-prized way station for travelers in this remote area, an attraction for visitors to the region and for a time even a safe haven for polygamists fleeing the law in neighboring Utah.

In 1907, the U.S. government established the Kaibab Paiute Indian Reservation on the lands surrounding Pipe Spring, which remained part of a privately owned ranch. Eventually, the owners agreed to cede the spring and

Winsor Castle to the public domain, and the former ranch became Pipe Spring National Monument in 1923. It remains an inviting oasis for travelers crossing the high-lonesome Strip, and it affords a fine window onto Arizona's past.

For more information

Pipe Spring National Monument
HC 65, Box 5
Fredonia, AZ 86022
(928) 643-7105
www.nps.gov/pisp

Vermilion Cliffs National Monument

It has been more than a century since California condors last flew over the Grand Canyon. The giant birds were once common throughout the Southwest, but for many reasons, including hunting and lead- and pesticide-poisoning, their numbers had fallen to only some 60 birds by the 1960s.

Thanks to an ambitious reintroduction program spearheaded by the Peregrine Fund in concert with state and federal wildlife agencies, *Gymnogyps californianus* graces the skies of northern Arizona again. On December 12, 1996, biologists released six captive-bred condors at the Vermilion Cliffs, near the eastern approach to the Grand Canyon, in the hope that the giants would multiply and reestablish themselves in their old habitat.

Initially, the great birds stayed close to the Vermilion Cliffs release site, which gives them plenty of room to roam. The remote 294,000-acre national monument, tucked away at the northeastern edge of the Kaibab Plateau and the Grand Canyon's North Rim, is a vast wonderland of stone, little visited even in the busiest seasons. Among its splendors are the cliffs themselves, named for their massive red wall of

ABOVE: The red stone of Winsor Castle glows at sunrise.
ROBERT G. McDONALD

TOP RIGHT: Hikers traverse the deep sandstone canyons of Vermilion Cliffs National Monument.
TOM BEAN

BOTTOM RIGHT: A balanced rock soaks up morning light before the Vermilion Cliffs, in the background.
ROBERT G. McDONALD

rock, that glows from afar, as well as Paria Canyon, a narrow slot canyon through which water perennially flows, an unusual thing in high-desert country.

The condors' numbers have grown, and their range has extended into the Grand Canyon proper and even farther west. They can be seen throughout the Colorado Plateau country. One particularly good spot for condor-watching skirts the western edge of the national monument: House Rock Valley Road (BLM Road 1065), a graded dirt surface, turns off of U.S. Route 89A and, after two miles, leads to the California Condor Viewing Site. The Vermilion Cliffs provide the condors a bit of condor paradise, a place in which we humans can find a bit of heaven, too.

For more information

Vermilion Cliffs National Monument
345 East Riverside Drive
St. George, UT 84790-6714
(435) 688-3200
www.blm.gov/az/vermilion/vermilion.htm

Grand Canyon-Parashant National Monument

The western edge of the Colorado Plateau, where the great sliver of land called the Arizona Strip meets the boundaries of Nevada and Utah, is wild, lonely country. In the old days, only a few hardy ranchers worked the land, while a few prospectors and explorers poked around in such ominously named places as Wolf Hole, Poverty Mountain, and Last Chance Canyon. Today, those places make up the Grand Canyon-Parashant National Monument, formally designated in January 2000.

The monument takes in 1,050,963 acres of spectacularly rugged country punctuated by forests of Joshua trees and broad desert washes, leading finally to Lake Mead and the westernmost portions of the Grand Canyon. Taking in the lower portion of the Shivwits Plateau, a watershed feeding the Colorado River through a series of deep side canyons, the monument is a geologist's dream, since for complex reasons the ancient rock formations have undergone less deformation than those elsewhere in the Grand Canyon region, giving a comparatively clear picture of the region's geological history. Taking in ecosystems that range from 1,000 to 8,000 feet in elevation, it is also the abode of many animal species, including condors, golden eagles, elk, mule deer, rattlesnakes, and whiptail lizards, as well as many different kinds of plants.

There are no visitor facilities within the monument, and the best of the roads are extremely primitive. Visitors should bring ample supplies of water, food, and gasoline; high-clearance, four-wheel-drive vehicles are recommended.

For more information

Grand Canyon-Parashant National Monument
345 East Riverside Drive
St. George, UT 84790-6714
(435) 688-3200
www.blm.gov/az/parashant/parashant.htm
www.nps.gov/para

TOP: The fluted sandstone of the Vermilion Cliffs dances its swirling ballet. DAVID ELMS JR.

ABOVE LEFT: A Joshua tree, the characteristic plant of the Mohave Desert, greets the night sky at Grand Canyon-Parashant National Monument. TOM BEAN

ABOVE RIGHT: At Pearce Ferry, west of Grand Canyon National Park, the calm water of Lake Mead glimmers. BRUCE GRIFFIN

White House Ruin, about 900 years old, hugs a sheer
cliff face in Canyon de Chelly. RANDY PRENTICE

the earth's
sacred
heart

canyon de chelly national monument

canyon de chelly national monument

oseph Campbell, the famed student of mythology and religion, once called Canyon de Chelly "the most sacred place on Earth." Carl Jung, the Swiss psychologist, who had a few ideas about mythology and religion himself, concurred. Besides, he added, Canyon de Chelly, a complex of wide canyons on the edge of the Defiance Plateau in northeastern Arizona, was the only place he knew outside of the Valley of the Nile that so truly embodied the very essence of antiquity.

Sacred and ancient the place is, to be sure. But I got the sense that change was coming to timeless, storied Canyon de Chelly when I visited there on a cold February morning in 1995. I was traveling on one of the giant balloon-tired, natural gas–fueled flatbed trucks frankensteined into tour buses that Navajo operators bring into the canyon year-round. The ungainly contraption decided to experience engine trouble below the White House Ruin, an Ancestral Puebloan cliff dwelling a thousand years old. As I sat on a rock ledge below the ruin and admired the view, a young Navajo man about my age, Adam Teller, came over. We nodded at each other, then sat without speaking for a couple of minutes, as is customary. Finally, gazing up at the ancient ruins, he said, "Do you know anything about the Internet?"

I had been working as a freelance editor for Amazon.com and had been boning up on all things cyberspace. "I'm no expert," I replied, "but I do quite a lot of my work these days online."

"Interesting," Adam replied. "I'm just learning how to write HTML. I'm going to put up a home page sometime this year to advertise my jewelry business."

I asked him where he lived, and he pointed to a hogan, a traditional Navajo octagonal house, nearby. I pointed out, helpfully, that it had no electricity, and Adam said, "I know. I thought about a satellite link and a generator to get around that problem, but that started running into big money. I'll just have to drive to Flagstaff every few days and check my e-mail on my friend's computer. It'll be good to keep track of my customers in Europe."

That was another bit of evidence to prove that it takes just one word to burst open a big balloon tire full of assumptions. Canyon de Chelly is a wonderful place to experience such things, and the Navajo people, blessed with both ancient wisdom and a droll, often deadpan sense of humor, are just the people to do the bursting.

I think of another wintry moment, standing at an overlook on the canyon's south rim, transfixed by the magnificence of the 800-foot-tall sandstone monolith called Spider Rock. Looking at it, you would believe that

OPPOSITE: Their leaves the gold of autumn, cottonwood trees line a wash in Canyon del Muerto. RANDY PRENTICE

BELOW LEFT: Water flows through Chinle Wash below Tsegi Overlook. JERRY SIEVE

BELOW RIGHT: Yucca, Mormon tea, and cholla line the rim of Canyon de Chelly at Tsegi Overlook. TOM DANIELSEN

only a spider could negotiate its heights, although it is said that humans have scaled it.

As I stood there, a Navajo man named Ronnie Nez came to share the view. After a few moments, he turned and said, "The Tribal Council just voted to ban hang gliding here."

"Well," I said, "the insurance load must have been pretty heavy."

"No, it wasn't that, really," Ronnie said. "It was just too expensive to hire medicine people to exorcise the ghosts every time someone crashed."

The Navajo word *Tséyi'*, of which Chelly is a Spanish approximation, means "within the rocks." The name is entirely fitting for this stony place, whose origin, a Navajo story has it, lay in a huge storm that once passed through what was then a gentle valley, tearing off the soil and grass and aspen trees. In the wake of the storm, tall, single pillars of rock stood on the valley floor, flanked by steep canyon walls of red rock, the Canyon de Chelly we know today.

Canyon de Chelly lies at the heart of the Navajo world, the *Diné Bekeyah*. Apart from a four-year period when U.S. cavalry troopers under Kit Carson removed most of the Navajos who lived there and marched them off into captivity,

burning their hogans and peach orchards in the bargain, the Navajo people have made their homes here for many generations. It is a fine testimonial to their generosity, particularly after that terrible episode, that the Navajos consented to having the canyon become part of the federal system of national parks and monuments (though it is not federally owned, but rather held by the Navajo Nation).

Occupying 131 square miles and established in 1931, Canyon de Chelly National Monument—which encompasses Canyon de Chelly, Canyon del Muerto, and Monument Canyon—is a place where some 200 Navajo families live, at least for part of the year. It also contains more than 1,500 known archaeological sites—some of which date back 5,000 years, lending authority to Campbell's and Jung's ideas about the ancientness of the place. Most of those sites mark spots where the forebears of some of today's Pueblo Indian peoples, sometimes known by the Navajo name Anasazi, lived; some of these structures, ranging from simple pit houses to many-storied pueblos, date to the 4th century.

The Navajos came to Canyon de Chelly sometime after the original Ancestral Puebloans

ABOVE: Potholes in the caprock at Canyon de Chelly's rim form miniature lakes after a rain. RANDY PRENTICE

RIGHT: White House Ruin, an Ancestral Puebloan architectural masterpiece, makes use of a natural alcove in a towering sandstone wall. TOM DANIELSEN

had migrated late in the 13th century, when a regional drought caused the small river within it to dry up for much of the year. Some of the Puebloans, historians conjecture, moved eastward to the Rio Grande, while others traveled westward to the Hopi Mesas and beyond. By the time the Navajo people arrived, the stream was flowing once again, at least for most of the year, exiting the canyon at the little town of Chinle, "where the water flows out." (Fittingly, Tsaile Creek has its headwaters in the Tunitcha Mountains, "where the water gathers.")

Visitors can get a sense of Canyon de Chelly's ancient history by following two scenic routes, the 36-mile-long (round trip) South Rim Drive, with seven overlooks, and the 34-mile-long (round trip) North Rim Drive, with four overlooks. On South Rim Drive, travelers come first to Tsegi Overlook, which offers a dizzying view down a 500-foot canyon face. White House Overlook offers access, via a 2.5-mile-long trail, to the heavily visited cliff dwelling where I met Adam Teller. A walker in reasonably good shape can make the trip in a couple of hours, though the trail is not for those bothered by heights or sheer drops.

At the end of South Rim Drive, Spider Rock Overlook takes in a view where the canyon walls fall off more than 1,000 feet, just across from the tall spire called Spider Rock. There, in Navajo belief, lives the master of another kind of web entirely. The sandstone pillar, which forks into two above the

canyon floor as if split by a mighty thunderclap, seems to be a magnet for wondrous weather, marked by lightning flashes and threatening clouds. Such tempestuous weather is just as it should be for a divine abode, the home of Spider Woman, a protector who, among other things, taught the ancestral Indians of Canyon de Chelly how to weave, a skill that would evolve after the Spanish arrived with their woolly sheep.

Navajo storytellers have much to say about Spider Woman, as do their neighbors, the Hopi people. Early one morning, while walking across the 15-foot-wide land bridge that links the mesa-top Hopi villages of Sichomovi and Walpi, I happened upon a young boy, 5 or 6 years old, leaning perilously over the edge, staring down a cliff face 500 feet tall. I asked him what he was looking at, and without looking up he said, "Spiders." It occurred to me only later that his grandmother must have told him tales of Spider Woman, said to kidnap unwary children, precisely in order to keep him safely away from such heights. It didn't work in this case. Like the unfortunate Arachne, the weaver who, the ancient Greeks said, spun her life away in a cave, Spider Woman is both a beloved and scary presence, just as is her home on that windswept, lightning-lashed monolith, one of the most striking places on Earth.

For its part, the North Rim Drive offers a view of Antelope House, located at the point where Canyon del Muerto and Black Rock Canyon come together. There, a Navajo artist

OPPOSITE: A rainbow, a symbol of life's journey, takes shape over rain-swept Spider Rock, a Canyon de Chelly landmark. GEORGE STOCKING

ABOVE: Spider Rock and the deep recesses of Canyon de Chelly wear a thick blanket of snow. LES DAVID MANEVITZ

ABOVE: Sunset shadows fill the depths where Canyon de Chelly (right) and Canyon del Muerto meet. TOM DANIELSEN

RIGHT: The Tower, now a ruin at Mummy Cave in Canyon del Muerto, was built a thousand years ago. GEORGE H.H. HUEY

drew a stunningly beautiful series of pictographs of running antelope, paintings that later inspired some of Adam Teller's subtle jewelry designs. Eight miles up the road is the famous Mummy Cave Overlook, giving a view of an ancient pueblo that owes its name to a group of mummified bodies found inside it. Nearby Massacre Cave Overlook is a reminder of more recent deaths, those of more than a hundred men, women, and children slaughtered by Spanish soldiers in 1805, an event that many Navajo people recall as if it were only yesterday.

But the best way to see Canyon de Chelly is from within. To do so, you will need to rent or bring your own four-wheel-drive vehicle and hire a Navajo guide; stop by the visitors center at the canyon's entrance to make arrangements. You can also take a motor tour of the canyon by signing on at the monument's Thunderbird Lodge, where delicious Navajo tacos await the intrepid traveler as a reward for taking in so much fresh air and so much history.

Daniel Staley, my guide, is teaching me to make a fire. Sitting beneath Antelope House, he takes strips of cottonwood bark, lays them against a log, and steadily scrapes one of them with a larger chip of cottonwood. Three minutes go by, then four, while Daniel talks, quietly, about the things his grandfathers taught him. And then a slender plume of smoke rises.

We have been traveling through Canyon de Chelly for a few hours, bouncing around in a truck along the sandy bed of a steadily narrowing wash, cracking our way over thick layers of ice. Normally, at this time of year, only a trickle of water flows through the wash, but up at the little town of Tsaile at the canyon's head, the reservoir is full of water from the steep, well-watered mountains, and so some of its supply has been freed to spill downstream. The result is that Canyon de Chelly's floor is a winter wonderland of thick, glittering ice that sends spectral beams of light into the dark-red corners of the canyon's high walls, illuminating their store of tucked-away caves and ancient rock dwellings.

When we set off early on this bright December morning, slipping and sliding along the wash, it was a scant 5 degrees above zero. We have been traveling slowly, steadily, up the ominously named Canyon del Muerto, "canyon of death," an 18-mile-long tributary of Canyon de Chelly. The sun has risen above the canyon's walls, filling in the valley floor with light, and it has warmed up to a crackling 28 degrees. Grateful for this newly arrived balminess, we stop below Antelope House to make an al fresco picnic of salami, cheese, apples, and chocolate, a perfect outdoor feast.

I study the edge of a rock overhang above, etched with a map of the night sky. I make out the W shape of Cassiopeia, what the Navajos call *náhookos ba'áádi*, and the Big Dipper, *náhookos bikhá'i*. Both figure prominently in the winter starscape, as does Venus. Their representations here, which Navajo artists scratched long ago into the crumbling sandstone alongside one of the canyon's best-preserved ruins, suggests the importance of the night sky to the ancient inhabitants of the Colorado Plateau. After all, the Ancestral Puebloans sited their cliff houses for many reasons, not only for ease of defense and proximity to productive agricultural fields, but also for the best possible views of the night sky, that infinite source of stories and metaphors. Indeed, just as the stars guided Europeans before we learned to let machines do our looking for us, the Ancestral Puebloans organized many of their lifeways around the heavens.

The Navajo knowledge of the stars is well attested to in Canyon de Chelly, where dozens of "planetaria" grace walls, ledges, and caves. The winter night sky is particularly well represented, since winter was traditionally a quiet time, the harvest in and stored and the planting yet to begin, a time

to make art and plan for the future. So it is in Canyon de Chelly today: Whereas dozens of Navajo farmers work the canyon during the productive months, only
two now live there in this quiet season.

We hear the whinnying of one of those farmers' horses, and a curl of smoke rises above a nearby hogan tucked into a spectacularly, explosively golden grove of cottonwood trees. Daniel walks up to me and says, "It's like church. This canyon is a sacred place to all the Navajo. When you come here, it clears your mind, and you go home strong. The canyon is our mother, and she feeds us."

Standing beneath the cottonwoods, their leaves rattling in a now soft wind, I understand.

Daniel sings softly:

We can chase my horse
We can chase my horse
In my Jeep Wrangler
In my Jeep Wrangler . . .
I can show you a shooting star
I can show you a shooting star
In my Jeep Wrangler
In my Jeep Wrangler . . .

The melody could be a thousand years old, rhythmic and gentle, echoing off the redwall cliffs, reverberating into every corner of the ancient ruin, rising high into the cold air, proclaiming how good it is to be alive. It is also very modern, like the Internet and hang gliders, a neat fit for the world of iPods and jet planes and satellite radio. That is the essence of Canyon de Chelly itself: a place that knows no time, that will always be here.

"May it be beautiful before me," the Navajo Night Chant asks of the heavens. "May I walk in beauty." Here in Canyon de Chelly, the Earth's sacred heart, that hopeful prayer is fulfilled.

Location

Approximately 350 miles northeast of Phoenix. From Phoenix, take Interstate 17 north to Interstate 40 at Flagstaff. Follow Interstate 40 east approximately 140 miles to Exit 333, Chambers/Ganado. Follow U.S. Route 191 38 miles to Ganado, where the road detours to State Route 264. Travel west approximately 6 miles, then reacquire U.S. 191. Continue north for 47 miles to Chinle. The entrance to Canyon de Chelly National Monument lies 2 miles east of Chinle on Indian Route 7.

Activities

Hiking, walking, bird-watching, horseback riding (by prior arrangement), camping (with a special-use permit only), four-wheel-drive tours. Check at the visitors center or at the Thunderbird Lodge, Holiday Inn Canyon de Chelly, or Best Western Canyon de Chelly Inn for guided tours and other programs.

For more information

Canyon de Chelly National Monument
P.O. Box 588
Chinle, AZ 86503
(928) 674-5500
www.nps.gov/cach

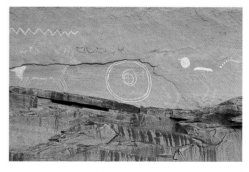

TOP LEFT: A hogan, the traditional octagonal Navajo house, offers warmth and shelter in a Canyon de Chelly winter. JERRY SIEVE

TOP RIGHT: Chinle Wash, "where the water comes out," gleams in autumn sunlight. GEORGE H.H. HUEY

ABOVE TOP: Navajo (in brown) and Ancestral Puebloan (in white) pictographs grace the canyon wall near Antelope House, Canyon del Muerto. GEORGE H.H. HUEY

ABOVE: Navajo petroglyphs, hundreds of years old, depict a chase on horseback. JERRY SIEVE

Hubbell Trading Post National Historic Site

In 1878, an entrepreneur from New Mexico, John Lorenzo Hubbell (1853-1930), set up shop in the small Navajo crossroads community of Ganado. He bought a trading post that was started two years earlier and was the only one around for many miles, and through it Hubbell brought food and goods—from needles and thread to wagon grease to seed corn—to the residents of far-flung settlements from Canyon de Chelly to Black Mesa and beyond. Hubbell was well-liked, and his broad network of friends and associates helped him enjoy a side career in politics, during which he was instrumental in Arizona's achieving statehood in 1912.

More important, Hubbell was a fair man who gave a good price, and Navajo weavers and silversmiths traveled long distances over the vast Navajo Nation to do business with him, trading craftwork such as fine silverwork, basketry, beadwork, and the famed Ganado red weavings for which the Hubbell Trading Post would become well-known. Indeed, Lorenzo Hubbell acted tirelessly as an agent and broker, helping popularize Navajo art far beyond the Southwest and even influencing the development of certain styles and techniques.

The trading post that bears his name was only part of Hubbell's small empire. At Ganado, he founded a smithy, making horseshoes and wagon fittings, as well as a freighting business and a 110-acre hay farm. Collectively, Hubbell's enterprises made for an important source of employment for the people of Ganado, and Hubbell proved himself a staunch ally of the Navajo people in many other ways as well.

Today, the Hubbell Trading Post, which became part of the national park system in 1967, remains influential in the world of Navajo art. It is also a fascinating memorial to Arizona's past, to a time before automobiles and telephones joined the remote Navajo Nation to the larger world.

For more information

Hubbell Trading Post National Historic Site
P.O. Box 150
Ganado, AZ 86505–0150
(928) 755-3475
www.nps.gov/hutr

TOP: The main building at Hubbell Trading Post, which has been an important center of Navajo commerce, dates to about 1883. GEORGE H.H. HUEY

ABOVE: A showcase for textiles and other traditional works of art, the Rug Room is filled with magnificent Navajo weavings. GEORGE H.H. HUEY

Navajo National Monument

Navajo National Monument, located near Monument Valley, comprises three Anasazi ruins: Betatakin, Keet Seel, and the now-closed Inscription House, the last so named for a date, 1661, scrawled on one of its walls by an unknown Spanish explorer.

An easy walk from a paved parking area, requiring about three hours round-trip, leads to Betatakin Ruin (which the Hopi people call *Talastima*), a large cliff house complex that seems almost to hang in midair before a sheer, high sandstone wall. Invulnerable to attack, the Betatakin complex was begun in about 1250, completed 40 years later, and then almost instantly abandoned. When it was discovered by a passing American rancher in 1907, the individual apartments were full of baskets, pottery, and preserved grains and ears of corn, almost as if its occupants had been chased away in the middle of a meal—which makes for quite a mystery.

The 17-mile trip to the slightly older Keet Seel (*Kawestima*) Ruin, its construction begun at the beginning of the 13th century, takes a full day on foot or horseback. Anyone who suffers from vertigo should avoid it, for it involves descending a narrow trail down a 1,100-foot, near-vertical rock face. Still, those who endure the trip will see yet another spectacular cliff dwelling that, unlike the more accessible ruins of Canyon de Chelly, is absolutely free of crowds. Its solitude invites reflection on its remarkable inhabitants and what made them flee their homelands so hastily.

To reach Navajo National Monument, follow U.S. Route 160 to the State Route 564 cutoff beyond Kayenta. A park service road leads to Navajo National Monument headquarters. The monument is so named, by the way, because it was the first federal park to be established on the grounds of the Navajo Nation, and not because of confusion over who built the great ruins.

For more information

Navajo National Monument
HC 71 Box 3
Tonalea, AZ 86044
(928) 672-2700
www.nps.gov/nava

TOP LEFT: A corrugated jar bears silent witness to the long-departed inhabitants of Keet Seel cliff dwelling. GEORGE H.H. HUEY

TOP RIGHT: Betatakin, another cliff dwelling within Navajo National Monument, was built in the 1200s. GEORGE H.H. HUEY

ABOVE: Shaded by a great rock overhang, Keet Seel offered its ancient makers shelter from the elements and enemies. RICK ODELL

Lithodendron Wash flows through the sandstone and clay hills of Petrified Forest National Park at sunset. JACK DYKINGA

# of constancy
and change

petrified forest national park

petrified forest national park

We humans begin our lives discovering the world one thing at a time: a face, a shape, a taste, a name. As we grow a little older, to the ripe age of four or five, having become familiar with many things, we start to take an interest in more exotic stuff. Thus, almost every child of that age, as the eminent naturalist E.O. Wilson has observed, goes through phases of enchantment with insects, snakes, birds, and, most exotic of all, dinosaurs. Wilson, who won a Nobel Prize for his work with ants, confesses to having never lost his passion for creepy-crawlies. For my part, I never lost mine for dinosaurs—one reason that I find Petrified Forest National Park, with its strange landforms and stranger roster of former inhabitants, to be such a wonderful place to haunt.

Petrified Forest is the only park in the national system devoted wholeheartedly to the Triassic period, when, 250 million years ago, ancestral reptiles emerged to become the kings of beasts. Preserving both dinosaur bones and the remains of giant trees that long ago turned to yellow, pink, purple, and green stone, the mile-high park takes in arid, sparsely vegetated landscapes of weathered rock and multicolored sand, places well suited for a science-fiction film set on some distant planet—and that look as if dinosaurs could be at home among them even today, not counting the wood-and-stucco ones on hillsides in the vicinity, fine specimens of homegrown whimsy.

Once upon a time, all those millions of years ago, the vast tableland called the Colorado Plateau was a swamp, crisscrossed by rivers and streams that provided ample nourishment for giant trees, ferns, and cycads. The climate was warm, the ground fertile, just the sort of place vegetarian dinosaurs such as *stagonolepis* and the prosauropods might think an earthly paradise. Doubtless the many species of bipedal carnivores and ancestral crocodiles, whose remains have been found in the park, found the area congenial, too, full of tasty creatures such as the hippopotamuslike *placerias* and the much smaller ancestral birds that once teemed here.

The park is less well known for its dinosaurs, though, than for its view into the environment that sheltered them. When they toppled, as all trees eventually must, the giant *araucarioxylon*, *woodworthia*, and *schilderia* that once grew here were eventually swallowed up by silt and mud, which kept the wood safe from the decaying effects of oxygen. Slowly, over the eons, silica—the stuff of which quartz and opal are made—replaced the wood tissue, leading to the strange sight of logs now made of gemlike stone.

There are petrified forests elsewhere in the world, but few are as extensive and well-preserved as this one. Added to the park's

OPPOSITE: A massive block of petrified wood adds its red tones to the blues of Blue Mesa. LARRY ULRICH

TOP: A natural bridge formed by a petrified log spans a snow-filled rivulet atop Blue Mesa. WILLARD CLAY

ABOVE: The Painted Desert, as seen from Chinde Point at the north end of Petrified Forest National Park, fills with dawn light. CHUCK LAWSEN

trove of past splendors is the natural beauty of the Painted Desert, of which Petrified Forest is but a small part. Recognizing the rarity of what was then known mostly to the hardy Arizonans of the high country, and urged on by the great naturalist John Muir, who lived at Petrified Forest for a few months on his way to the redwoods of California, President Theodore Roosevelt set aside a small portion of the present park as a national monument in 1906. In 1932, the monument grew in size, and tracts of wilderness in the Painted Desert fell into its boundaries after the monument became a national park in 1962. At last count it measured 218,533 acres, full of diverse wonders that have rewarded generations of visitors.

Not all of those wonders lie in antiquity. Though it is dedicated to the remains of a remote past, Petrified Forest is in every way a living park. Its forests, grasslands, desert plains, and stream and river valleys are home to hundreds of plant, bird, mammal, reptile, and insect species, some of them not often seen elsewhere. I have enjoyed the park in every season, but I have to confess to liking it best in

spring, when the weather is warming and all those creatures and plants are stirring, greeting the season with exuberant growth and an extraordinary amount of hustle and bustle. All of this makes the park a wonderful destination for wildlife watchers and wildflower enthusiasts as well as dinosaur buffs.

Enter the park on a lovely April day, and you'll find blooming evening primroses, Indian paintbrush, mariposa lilies, sunflowers, snakeweed, rabbitbrush, buckwheat, peppergrass, and saltbush lining the park's roads and trails, awakening to the new season. The animals are quickening, too; at any given moment you'll likely find a roadrunner waiting to race, a turkey vulture floating lazily along on the thermal winds, a tarantula scurrying across the ancient ocean floor, and perhaps even a porcupine stretching out its spiny back and pondering the day's plans.

One of Petrified Forest's most visible denizens is the Gunnison's prairie dog (*Cynomys gunnisoni*), one of five prairie dog species in the United States. Prairie dogs are few in their formerly broad range, but within the park they find

OPPOSITE: A confusion of petrified wood carpets the slopes of Blue Mesa. LAURENCE PARENT
ABOVE: The sediment hills and petrified logs of Blue Mesa glow in early morning light. RANDY PRENTICE

the hospitality of a natural grassland unbroken by fences and undisturbed by grazing, a place ideally suited to their kind. Weighing in at two to four pounds, a good size as rodents go, the Gunnison's take their hibernation seriously, disappearing below ground at the first sign of cold weather and there going about the business of producing the next year's batch of young. In the early spring, when the pups, just weeks old, emerge from under ground with their parents, their colonies become antic playgrounds full of little heads popping up everywhere, busily going from mound to mound.

Of the six established colonies within the national park, three are easily accessible from the main road. The first, and largest, is just off Exit 311 on Interstate 40, at the park's northern entrance. The colony numbers several hundred individuals, though just how many depends on the severity of the winter and other environmental factors. Other prairie dog colonies, also called coteries, lie just beyond Long Logs, near the southern entrance to the park, and at Newspaper Rock, which stands at the center of the park and commands a fine view of the Puerco River valley and the oddly shaped rock formations called The Tepees.

Having lived next to a large colony of them as a child, I confess to a great fondness for prairie dogs. My feelings are evidently shared by the many wildlife biologists who come to the park to study its population, made up of inquisitive, even friendly, prairie dogs who seem to have no particular fear of humans. What is more, the prairie dogs turn out to be extraordinarily communicative and social among their own kind, greeting one another with what looks like a kiss—a phenomenon that puzzled biologists, inasmuch as prairie dogs elsewhere behave with a touch more reserve. The prairie dogs aren't exactly kissing, in fact, but rubbing their front teeth together, which to a rodent must have the same friendly effect. Whatever the case, every prairie dog in the park has a keen sense of belonging and of social obligation. Thus it is that when trouble comes, as it so often does, one will sound an alarm, an unmistakably urgent "chirk-chirk-chirk" sound until all of its fellows are safely underground. When the source of trouble leaves, another prairie dog will sound an all-clear signal, whereupon the prairie dogs celebrate with what biologists call a "jump-yip," which is just that: a vigorous arching of the back, a spring in the air, and a triumphant bark. Who wouldn't be proud, even ecstatic, after all, to stare danger in the face and live to tell the tale?

The Gunnison's get a lot of practice at all this, for find a prairie dog, and a golden eagle is likely to be nearby, hoping to find a convenient meal. Fearsome from a small rodent's point of view and impressive by any measure, with their 8-foot wingspans and sharp talons, the eagles patrol the ground throughout the park, but they're especially numerous at Long Logs and Newspaper Rock. Joining them are other skilled hunters; in the morning and evening, prime time for chasing game, the sky is alive with American kestrels, prairie falcons, and red-tailed hawks, and the ground empty of all but the most incautious mice, pocket gophers, kangaroo rats, white-tailed antelope squirrels, cottontail rabbits, and, of course, prairie dogs. To us humans, they don't cut quite the same fearsome figure as a giant ancestral crocodile, but I imagine that the park's abundant raptor population was reason enough for the prairie dogs to agree to cooperate in the face of so much danger. Perhaps, over the passage of years, the other creatures here will follow suit and take the same us-against-the-world precautions.

A less vigorous hunter, the raven makes its home throughout the park as well. These birds are noisy under any circumstance, but even more so when visitors approach, because visitors mean food. It's no accident that these highly intelligent, social birds gather at just the spots where humans do, at roadside picnic tables and the parking lots leading to heavily visited places such as the Agate Bridge and Crystal Forest. Take a sandwich out of a hamper and you'll find that you've drawn a cawing crowd of onlookers, waiting for a shot at a convenient lunch. But don't be fooled and give in to the ravens' demands to be fed, for feeding any animal here is a definite no-no. It may take a heart as hard as petrified wood to refuse their croaked entreaties for food, but there's no need to feel sorry for the ravens: Except in deepest winter, there is always a fresh crop of insects nearby, and the birds don't lack for meals.

Other avian species add their songs, whistles, and wingbeats to the air: here a northern mockingbird, there a bluebird, a brightly colored western tanager or kingbird, or a chattering house finch. Seasoned

ABOVE: Ancient petroglyphs tell a story of life at Petrified Forest. WILLARD CLAY

RIGHT: Snow carpets the glistening multicolored stones of the appropriately named Agate Forest. WILLARD CLAY

bird-watchers will have added these species to their life lists long ago, but Petrified Forest draws plenty of bird-watchers just the same, for it sees a dazzling parade of migratory species passing through, as birds such as Virginia rails, herons, egrets, geese, wigeons, ibises, and even pelicans make their way to better-watered and greener places far away.

Resident year-round are the pronghorns, often (but mistakenly) called "antelopes," deerlike animals that feed on sagebrush and grasses that grow abundantly on the plain alongside the Puerco River. If you catch sight of a pale blur against the multicolored rocks of the park, the chances are good that you're seeing a pronghorn. With its distinctive white rump and curled horns, *Antilocapra americana* is the fastest land animal in North America, clocking speeds at up to 70 miles an hour and covering the ground in 20-foot leaps and bounds. Whether on the go or at rest, pronghorns are easy to pick out in the open terrain. Look for them browsing along the railroad track that crosses the northern end of the park—or, if it's raining or windy, in the gullies and washes that comb the river valley, where they like to shelter. Lithodendron Wash, which branches off from the northwestern end of the park, is a good place to find them in such weather. Smaller herds also graze below Blue Mesa and Agate Mesa farther down the road, and I have often been thrilled to find them running alongside my vehicle—but only for an instant, for there's no speed limit governing their movement.

As befits a place famous for its long-ago population of dinosaurs, Petrified Forest has a varied resident population of reptiles. Collared lizards scamper about everywhere you look. Side-blotched lizards race along ancient fallen logs. Striped whiptails, seemingly as fast as pronghorns, add another blur to the view. The kingsnake, with its alternating bands of black and white, light brown, or yellow, is common and is sometimes seen in pursuit of another resident, the Western rattlesnake—for the kingsnake seems to think nothing of its fellow snake's venom and to enjoy a meal of rattler whenever the opportunity presents itself. If you're patient, and lucky, you may see another of the park's venomous reptiles, the shy and altogether rare Hopi rattlesnake, a sensitive species in more ways than one—so be sure to give it a wide berth. I like to think that the rattler bites only those who would even consider, even for the most fleeting of moments, pocketing even the littlest piece of petrified wood as a souvenir, another definite no-no. Of course, by that criterion, you and I would never find ourselves in danger of being bitten.

Rare, too, is the badger, a creature honored in Zuni, Navajo, and Hopi art but not often seen in the wild. So uncommon is *Taxidea taxus*, in fact, that most park employees have never seen one. Still, good things come to those who wait, and park rangers say that the best place to spot one of these slow-moving animals is the area around Blue Mesa, where several sightings have been recorded in the last few years. Badgers also have been seen from time to time at Newspaper Rock and along the Painted Desert rim just outside the north visitors center, so keep an eye out for them.

TOP: Petrified Forest National Park takes in many landforms, including eroded badlands and broad plains. TOM DANIELSEN

LEFT: The moon sets over the Long Logs section of Petrified Forest. LARRY ULRICH

When night falls and most of its human visitors leave, a profound stillness descends on Petrified Forest. Skinny and hungry after the long winter, coyotes are abundant indeed, as are the black-tailed jackrabbits that they chase. Plentiful, too, are the Western spotted and the striped skunks, shy of humans and well-equipped to ward off danger with their awful perfume. The nighttime sky, spangled with stars, is the province of horned and long-eared owls, which take over the work of patrolling the air from the now-resting hawks and eagles, and of bats, which greet the spring in astonishing numbers. Nesting in caves, rock overhangs, and even the garages of park employees, the California myotis, small-footed myotis, pallid, and Western pipistrelle bats live in the park year-round, joined by the occasional little brown, hoary, Brazilian free-tailed, and silver-haired varieties, all of which feast on the insects that rise from the trees and grasses as the ground cools.

Petrified Forest embodies whole worlds, the vibrant and the long dead, the distant past and the onrushing present, the unchanging constant mixed with the constantly changing. At almost any time of the year that you choose to visit, whether to see the remains of giant trees or to commune with fleet-footed pronghorns, you'll be greeted by a tuneful symphony of whirring wings, of canine howls, of cawing ravens and barking prairie dogs. Listen closely, standing among those fantastic bejeweled trees in this remarkable landscape, and you may just hear the keening of Triassic ghosts as well, longing for the days when dinosaurs ruled this land. That's the stuff of which childhood dreams are born, dreams to last a lifetime.

Location

Approximately 230 miles northeast of Phoenix. From Phoenix, take Interstate 17 north to Flagstaff. There follow Interstate 40 east to Exit 311, about 24 miles east of Holbrook. The park entrance and visitors center are just to the north of the interstate; the 28-mile road through the park begins there and ends at the southern entrance off U.S. Route 180.

Activities

Hiking, walking, bird-watching. Check at the visitors center for nature walks and other programs. Both park entrances have shops offering food, drink, and other items. Elsewhere the park has no services, so carry water and snack food. Wear sturdy shoes for walking along the park trails. Please note that federal law prohibits collecting plants, rocks, fossils, and petrified wood, and feeding or transporting wildlife.

For more information

Petrified Forest National Park
P.O. Box 2217
Petrified Forest, AZ 86028
(928) 524-6228
www.nps.gov/pefo

TOP: The Long Logs glow in the rising sun. GEORGE H.H. HUEY

ABOVE LEFT: A Gunnison's prairie dog, one of Petrified Forest's most visible and valued citizens, stands guard over his populous colony. C.K. LORENZ

ABOVE RIGHT: A desert mariposa lily opens in springtime, showing that Petrified Forest is a living park as well as one that preserves the ancient past. MARK S. SKALNY

ancient places and the sinagua world

The weathered stones of Wupatki National Monument bask in the warm light after a summer thunderstorm. GEORGE H.H. HUEY

sunset crater volcano national monument,
wupatki national monument,
walnut canyon national monument,
tuzigoot national monument, and
montezuma castle national monument

45

MONUMENTAL PLACES

sunset crater volcano national monument, wupatki national monument, walnut canyon national monument, tuzigoot national monument, and montezuma castle national monument

mountains form over unfathomably long periods of time. What were once ancient seafloors shed their waters, rise inch by inch, accumulate layers of sand and stone, warp and buckle with the movement of the earth over millions and millions of years. What were once ancient highlands, conversely, slowly weather away, ground down by the forces of wind and water and gravity, their stones washed away to line the floors of rivers and oceans, there to begin the mountain-building journey anew.

But if mountains take eons to rise, they can sometimes fall in the blink of an eye, geologically speaking. Forming a giant strato volcano resembling Japan's Mount Fuji or Tanzania's Mount Kilimanjaro, Arizona's San Francisco Mountains, which began forming about 1 million years ago, loomed to a height of more than 16,000 feet, higher than all but a few North American mountains today. About 400,000 years ago the east flank of that huge mountain may have erupted in a blast that tore the cone apart, spreading debris across the surrounding countryside. The explosion formed the great semicircular crater known as the Inner Basin, smoothed and shaped by later generations of glaciers, while the mountain continued to grumble and rumble for eons and to send out seismic spasms until as recently as 700 years ago.

The remaining mountain core, now marked by three jagged summits instead of one and covering an area of nearly 2,000 square miles, now stands half a mile lower than its ancestor, but it is still impressive by any standards, rising a mile above a surrounding high plateau that is itself nearly a mile and a half tall. At 12,633 feet in height, Humphreys Peak remains the highest point in Arizona, followed closely by its nearby sisters Agassiz Peak (12,356 feet) and Fremont Peak (11,969 feet), forming a rocky crown that is clearly visible from more than a hundred miles away—one reason that many Native American peoples, including the Hopi, Navajo, Western Apache, Yavapai, Hualapai, and Havasupai, consider the San Francisco Peaks of northern Arizona to be sacred and have long made their homes within sight of them.

The ancestors of the Zuni and Hopi people, among others, were within sight of those holy mountains when, somewhere between A.D. 1064 and 1067, a new eruption to the east occurred, creating Sunset Crater Volcano. Known as the Sinagua—Spanish for "without water," the name a Spanish explorer gave the area around Flagstaff, Arizona, which lacks permanent streams—this ancient people, archaeologists conjecture, began to migrate eastward from the Mojave Desert into the Arizona highlands about 2,000 years ago. In the desert, they had lived in low huts

OPPOSITE: The ancient pueblo of Wupatki sits in a bowl of rock, well hidden from ancient enemies. DAVID W. LAZAROFF

TOP: The San Francisco Peaks tower over a field of blue larkspur and yellow goldenrod. CHUCK LAWSEN

ABOVE: The San Francisco Peaks show a different visage in winter, with their deep mantle of snow. CHUCK LAWSEN

ABOVE: Montezuma Well, a limestone sink fed by perennial springs, was an important center for the ancient Sinagua people. GEORGE H.H. HUEY

called *jacals* and, as nomads, had accumulated few material things, the stuff of which archaeology is made. Almost nothing is known of them prior to coming to live under the shadow of the San Francisco Peaks. Then, probably influenced by the architecturally sophisticated Ancestral Puebloans to the east, the Sinagua people began to expand their building styles, moving from reed huts to pit houses and then, in time, into great stone pueblos such as can be found at Wupatki National Monument.

The eruptions at Sunset Crater must have been terrifying, and it doubtless inspired Sinagua storytellers to spin great legends of the shaking, fire-spitting earth. But it also had a happy consequence, for the ashfall and lava flows created rich farmland where none had existed before. The Sinagua community flourished, as the ruins of Wupatki, with its extensive, many-roomed pueblos, ballcourt, and other structures, tell us. So, too, do the things found in those buildings, including goods from as far away as California, central Mexico, and the Rio Grande: seashells, obsidian blades, copper bells. A hundred years after the eruption, perhaps 5,000 Sinagua lived in the neighborhood of the pueblos and farmed the mesas and valleys surrounding Wupatki. They came to differentiate themselves by organizing their society around clans headed by women, and they developed traditions of stone-work and metalwork and basket-making, the products of which were widely traded among their neighbors.

Sunset Crater still rumbled and shook from time to time, but that had nothing to do with the eventual collapse of Wupatki. Sometime around the mid-13th century, a great drought descended on the Colorado Plateau, and large-scale farming in support of a large, centralized population became impractical. Clan by clan, we can imagine, the people of Wupatki began to drift away, some heading north and west toward the Grand Canyon, some wandering east to the Hopi mesas and beyond, where they would found new towns and continue to elaborate on the religious, cultural, and artistic traditions that we know and admire today.

The English writer Rose Macauley deemed "the pleasure of ruins" one of the great rewards of travel. Few voyagers standing among the broken limestone of the Roman Forum or gazing up at the Great Wall of China would dispute her remark, for there is something, after all, in being alive in the midst of long-dead cultures, in sensing the majesty of time. I have taken pleasure in ruins for so many years, traveling to such places as Xian, China, to see the terra-cotta warriors and southern Italy to see temples built by the ancient Greeks thousands of years ago. It is much less spectacular, but for many reasons the Sinagua settlement of Walnut Canyon is one of my favorite ruins anywhere, a complex of cliff dwellings built about the same time as Wupatki and abandoned in the mid-13th century as well.

Walnut Canyon was a favorite haunt of the writer Willa Cather, too, who spent parts of 1912 and 1915 (when the pueblo became a national monument) exploring the cliff dwellings. As she noted of the place she called Panther Canyon in her novel *The Song of the Lark*, the canyon walls made a natural defense, while the "deep groove running along the sides of the canyon" made a natural shelter inside which the Sinagua built tidy houses of stone and mortar on either side of the deep ravine. As Cather writes,

"The dead city had thus two streets, one set in either cliff, facing each other across the ravine, with a river of blue air between them. . . . The canyon twisted and wound like a snake, and these two streets went on for four miles or more, interrupted by the abrupt turnings of the gorge, but beginning again within each turn. The canyon had dozens of these false endings near its head. Beyond, the windings were larger and less perceptible, and it went on for a hundred miles, too narrow, precipitous, and terrible for man to follow it. The Cliff Dwellers liked wide canyons, where the great cliffs caught the sun. Panther Canyon had been deserted for hundreds of years when the first Spanish missionaries came into Arizona, but the masonry of the houses was still wonderfully firm; had crumbled only where a landslide or a rolling boulder had torn it."

The 80-odd dwellings of Walnut Canyon hang on the precipice of the world, spectacular and a touch mysterious. I am not easily given to supernatural feelings, but with its quiet and deep shadows, this is a place

TOP RIGHT: Sunflowers and billowing clouds frame a distant but still imposing Sunset Crater. TOM BEAN

MIDDLE: Montezuma Castle, tucked into a sandstone cliff face above the Verde Valley, stands about 100 feet above the valley floor, offering its occupants shelter and protection. GEORGE H.H. HUEY

BOTTOM: The deep recesses of Walnut Canyon harbor some 80 Sinagua dwellings, including this sturdy stone structure. TOM DANIELSEN

that lends itself well to thoughts of spirits and ghosts, of which Cather's protagonist entertained a few.

The place was already essentially waterless, requiring trips down to Walnut Creek hundreds of feet below, and the farming was practiced on a much smaller scale than at Wupatki. Was it fear of another explosion that drove the Sinagua to settle in such an unsettled—and even unsettling—locale in the first place? Was it the arrival of enemies from distant lands that made them seek the shelter of the cliffs? Or was it only the spectacular view, the easy access to water, trade routes, and game about which an ancient real estate agent might have boasted? We may never know.

Far below Walnut Canyon, in the fertile country below the Mogollon Rim, another branch of the Sinagua people had been farming for several hundred years. They, too, had moved from pit houses to pueblos, though their cultural influences tended to come from the Hohokam people of the southern desert, with whom they developed a flourishing trade. As these southern Sinagua developed traditions of textiles, jewelry making, and ceramics, their economy and numbers grew, and they founded several new settlements while expanding old ones. One very ancient settlement, with signs of human presence dating back 11 millennia, is to be found at the place that early Anglo settlers dubbed Montezuma Well—all things ancient in the Southwest, the assumption held, having been built by the faraway Aztecs. Sacred to the Yavapai and Hopi peoples, the great well is a limestone sink fed by deep underground springs that provide it with more than a million and a half

Tuzigoot National Monument, commanding the crown of a hill above agricultural fields, clearly served as a fortress for the ancients. TOM TILL

gallons of water every single day, a natural treasure in a dry land. That water flows through fissures in the limestone wall into Beaver Creek, which in turn empties into the Verde River, a tributary of the distant Gila River.

Though the chronology is spotty, it is believed that the southern Sinagua made Montezuma Well an important part of their domain early on, as the small pueblo on the wall of the well suggests. Another pueblo stood atop the hill above the limestone pit, with defensive walls made of limestone and sandstone, and at their height both villages would have numbered several hundred residents, large settlements in this part of the world.

The presence of so much wealth, natural and created, must have been a temptation for enemies, for in the 12th century the southern Sinagua began to build distinctively fortresslike structures on hilltops. Most were small, serving as signal towers along a troubled frontier; as you travel out of the Verde Valley, you can see their rubble on nearly every rise. Far larger was the village called Tuzigoot, on the crown of a low hill overlooking the meandering Verde River, which lends the pueblo its Apache name, meaning "crooked water." Numbering about 75 apartments, the two-story pueblo was clearly made for protection; the ruins reveal only a few doorways, and the Sinagua inhabitants had to enter or exit by means of ladders that were pulled up behind them.

Initially, founded in about 1125, Tuzigoot numbered only four dozen or so permanent residents, but as the Sinagua population grew, it came to number several hundred people by about 1400, all living in very close quarters. The present ruins resemble the sheepfolds of the western Irish coast, at least to my eye, but had no such peaceful origin. They hint at hard times, but no hard evidence of wide-scale warfare, of the sort that would come to plague the Yavapai people, has yet turned up.

Just so, the great five-story pueblo called Montezuma Castle, located on Beaver Creek, downstream of Montezuma Well, began to rise early in the 12th century. The imposing, handsome pueblo, built into a hollow in a limestone wall, stands about a hundred feet off the valley floor, making it easily defensible. All these centuries later, it is still impressive to behold. A larger, now badly deteriorated pueblo called Castle A, made up of about 45 rooms, stands a couple of hundred feet to the west, at the foot of the cliff.

TOP: Tuzigoot National Monument takes its name from the Apache phrase for "crooked water," the winding Verde River below. GEORGE H.H. HUEY

MIDDLE: Sunset Crater absorbs the intense light of a desert sunset. LARRY ULRICH

BOTTOM: Lomaki Ruin, part of Wupatki National Monument, glows in the first sun of day, with the snowcapped San Francisco Peaks in the distance. ROBERT G. McDONALD

The Sinagua residents of Montezuma Castle may have used the latter structure for their year-round residence, retreating to the higher levels in times of emergency, or they may have occupied both structures at all times. Like so much else about the Sinagua world, we simply don't know—though we do know for certain that Montezuma Castle was no longer inhabited a full century before its namesake was born.

In the early 15th century, like their cousins to the north, the southern Sinagua began to abandon the region and were likely assimilated into other peoples, perhaps among them the neighboring Yavapai and Apache. Why their civilization fell is a subject of debate. Some scholars have suggested the arrival of new enemies, others disease, still others internal strife verging on civil war. It must have been a terrible time for the Sinagua people, whatever the cause. They are long silent, and we know those ancient Arizonans mostly through the rocky, ghostly places in which they lived, which today number some of the greatest gems in the national park system.

Locations

Sunset Crater Volcano National Monument and Wupatki National Monument: The entrance to Sunset Crater Volcano and Wupatki National Monuments lies approximately 12 miles north of Flagstaff. Take U.S. Route 89 north and exit east at the sign. A loop road takes visitors to Sunset Crater Visitors Center (2 miles), Wupatki Visitors Center (21 miles), and continues out to a second junction with U.S. 89 after 35 miles.

Walnut Canyon National Monument: From Flagstaff, follow Interstate 40 east for 7.5 miles to Exit 204, with signs to the monument entrance. Follow the paved road south 3 miles to the visitors center.

Tuzigoot National Monument: About 90 miles from Phoenix; take Interstate 17 to Exit 287 and travel west on State Route 260 to Cottonwood. In Cottonwood, take Main Street north toward Clarkdale and follow signs to the monument.

Montezuma Castle National Monument and Montezuma Well: About 90 miles from Phoenix; take Interstate 17 to Exit 289. Follow the signs 3 miles to the monument. For Montezuma Well, a detached unit of Montezuma Castle National Monument, take Interstate 17 to Exit 293, and follow the paved and dirt road approximately 4 miles to the visitor check-in.

Activities

All these national monuments offer hiking trails; some have interpretive trails, camping facilities, and other amenities and offer programs on the natural and human history of the region.

For more information

Sunset Crater Volcano National Monument
Wupatki National Monument
Walnut Canyon National Monument
6400 North Highway 89
Flagstaff, AZ 86004
(928) 526-1157
Sunset Crater: www.nps.gov/sucr
Wupatki: www.nps.gov/wupa
Walnut Canyon: www.nps.gov/waca

Montezuma Castle National Monument
Tuzigoot National Monument
P.O. Box 219
Camp Verde, AZ 86322
(928) 567-5276
Montezuma Castle: www.nps.gov/moca
Tuzigoot: www.nps.gov/tuzi

TOP LEFT: Twiggy saplings break through the cinders of the Bonita Lava Flow, Sunset Crater Volcano National Monument. DAVID W. LAZAROFF

TOP RIGHT: As seen from the distance, the cliff dwellings of Walnut Canyon blend readily with their surroundings. RANDY PRENTICE

MIDDLE: Ponderosa pine cones rest on volcanic cinders at Sunset Crater. RANDY PRENTICE

BOTTOM: Aspen leaves come to rest on the cinders of Sunset Crater. GEORGE H.H. HUEY

Tonto National Monument

The Colorado Plateau ends in the sheer cliff wall called the Mogollon Rim, which marks the boundary between Arizona's high country and the lower deserts. There, below that river-laced edge, in the transitional country where pine trees and cacti meet not far from the shores of today's Roosevelt Lake, stands Tonto National Monument, preserving the ruins of cliff dwellings built eight centuries ago by the Salado people, the people of the Salt River and its environs.

Archaeologists conjecture that the Salado, a farming people, were an offshoot of the southerly Hohokam, a people whose past is preserved at Casa Grande Ruins National Monument. By about 1150, the Salado had diverged from Hohokam traditions, having come into contact with and absorbing influences from groups such as the Sinagua, Ancestral Puebloans, and Mogollon. They had to adapt all those influences to a land that, while rich, was also remote and difficult to travel through. As John Gregory Bourke, an American cavalry officer, wrote, the Tonto Basin "is a basin only in the sense that it is all lower than the ranges enclosing it—the Mogollon, the Mazatzal, and the Sierra Ancha—but its whole triangular area is so cut up by ravines, arroyos, small stream beds and hills of very good height, that it may safely be pronounced one of the roughest spots on the globe."

The Salado people arrived in the Tonto Basin at about the same time and immediately began building two great cliff dwellings, called the Upper and Lower Ruin. The former is an extensive structure containing about 40 dwellings; the latter has 16 rooms on the ground floor, three with upper stories. The Salado lived here for about three centuries, and then, between A.D. 1400 and 1450, they suddenly left, abandoning their cliff dwellings. No one knows why.

For more information

Tonto National Monument
HC 02 Box 4602
Roosevelt, AZ 85545
(928) 467-2241
www.nps.gov/tont

Agua Fria National Monument

Naturalists called the rugged country where the Sonoran Desert rises to meet the Mogollon Rim by many names, of which the Transition Zone and Central Highlands are the most common. Whatever the region is called, the jumble of mountains, mesas, and canyons that makes up Agua Fria National Monument, whose southern boundary lies only half an hour's drive north of Phoenix, is some of Arizona's least explored and least known country.

Designated as a national monument only in 2000, Agua Fria—its name derives from that of an intermittent river that flows through it and means "cold water" in Spanish—contains a vast number of archaeological sites that represent a mix, or at least a meeting, of the prehistoric Salado, Hohokam, and Sinagua cultures. About 450 such sites have been catalogued, but more await discovery. What is certain is that, as it is more thoroughly explored, the monument will enrich our understanding of Arizona's past, as well as our appreciation for how desert and highland plant and animal communities meet and adapt to ever-challenging circumstances.

Though a major highway, Interstate 17, runs along its western edge, a visit to Agua Fria is fundamentally a wilderness experience. The evocatively named Bloody Basin Road is a bumpy, rocky path best suited to four-wheel-drive, high-clearance vehicles; other roads are even bumpier, and even the main route from the monument down to the little town of Bumble Bee can be a challenge. The monument, as with the region as a whole, is subject to extremes of temperature. It is a place of flash floods, lightning, and venomous reptiles, of mountain lions and coyotes, of unmarked trails and long-abandoned wildcat mines.

In short, it's the untamed Arizona of old, a fascinating place that requires attention and planning, and that will reward the visitor with unforgettable sights and experiences.

For more information

Agua Fria National Monument
BLM Hassayampa Field Office
21605 North 7th Avenue
Phoenix, AZ 85027
(623) 580-5500
www.blm.gov/az/aguafria/pmesa.htm

TOP: Thick stone walls a sturdy roof, long fallen into disrepair, once sheltered the Salado inhabitants of Tonto National Monument. JERRY SIEVE

LEFT: A band of cottonwood and willow trees hugs a desert stream deep within Agua Fria National Monument. TOM BEAN

in the
land of
little rain

saguaro national park

saguaro national park

h *ahshani Bahithag Mashath*, "the moon of the saguaro cactus fruit." So the Tohono O'odham, the native people of the Sonoran Desert, call June, the onset of summer.

Every June for as long as memory can recall, the Desert People have come together, village by village, to harvest sweet red fruit from the tall tops of *Carnegeia gigantea*, the giant saguaro cactus. The height of the harvest coincides with the feast day of St. John the Baptist on June 24, when, local tradition holds, the first monsoon rains arrive. The Desert People gather the fruit to eat fresh—it tastes something like a cross between a cucumber and a sweet watermelon—and to make a fast-fermented wine, *nawait*, that they use to invoke the rain that gives this place life. Anthropologists call the process "sympathetic magic": a Tohono O'odham adult will drink enough of the slightly acrid wine to induce vomiting. Spilling from mouth to ground, the discharged wine encourages the rain to follow its lead, to pour from the clouds to the dry desert below.

The idea may seem unpleasant to some moderns, but so far the magic has worked: The Tohono O'odham have endured, and so has the saguaro, as can be seen in every corner of Saguaro National Park. It may not often rain on June 24, for the arrival of rain has been pushed later into the summer calendar in these last couple of comparatively dry decades, but that has not diminished the ancestral regard for the giant cacti, which take on such humanlike

forms—from the roads passing through either branch of the park, on either flank of the desert metropolis of Tucson, you can see them gathering in families, embracing, waving hello—that the Desert People consider them to be in the same domain as humans, and hold any crime committed against a saguaro as equivalent to some evil done against a person.

And so, in June, Tohono O'odham grownups raise their cups to their fellow beings, those tall, spiny, green cacti, awaiting the gift of rain from the heavens. The hot air accumulates, gathering force, drawing tiny droplets of water from the Sea of Cortés. The children sing rain songs, lovely invocations for the clouds to come and bestow their blessings. The Tohono O'odham poet Ofelia Zepeda, born in the dense saguaro forest of Quijotoa, offers a translation of one such song:

And somewhere along the way I stopped again
And it was my cloud that reached me
And it was sprinkling wetly
And here I reached your rainhouse and looked in
There lay many winds, there lay many clouds,
*   there lay many seeded things*
And you set them down and sat upon them
And with them I touched you
And you moved and breathed your wind
And with it were doing things
Here you dropped it upon my land
And with that my land was sprinkled
*   with water and was finished.*

OPPOSITE: Summer lightning flickers above the hills that ring Saguaro National Park. CHUCK LAWSEN

BELOW: Brittlebush and saguaros share the Red Hills, in the western section of Saguaro National Park. LES DAVID MANEVITZ

BELOW RIGHT: An antelope squirrel negotiates a spiny cholla bud. G.C. KELLY

ABOVE: A collared peccary, or javelina, stops to snack on a convenient prickly pear pad. G.C. KELLY

ABOVE RIGHT: Hohokam petroglyphs relate a long-ago story on the flank of Signal Hill. RANDY PRENTICE

The saguaro cactus is one of the defining species of the Sonoran Desert, along with the paloverde and ironwood trees and other denizens such as the coral snake and the Sonoran Desert toad. Together, these define the extent of the Sonoran Desert. At the desert's southern border, near the beautiful old colonial town of Alamos, Mexico, you'll find the stately cactus in dense growths alongside tropical plants; at the desert's northern edge, you'll see saguaros standing like solitary guards in bone-dry sand. The ecosystems are very different, but the saguaro still draws in much the same crowd of dependents wherever it may root: cactus wrens and burrowing owls nest in its trunk, saguaro bark beetles gnaw at its undergrowth, white-winged sphinx moths flutter about its flowers, and rodents feed upon its new growth, or "pups."

This desert is vast, and ancient. Now, when we say "desert," we mean, simply put, a place where the absence of readily available water (overall, the Sonoran Desert receives about 10 inches of rainfall a year) restricts the kind of life forms that inhabit it. Still, despite its rigors, the Sonoran Desert—made up of grasslands and thornscrub, dune fields and cactus forests, tree-lined rivers and sere lava pavements—is an overflowing ecological treasury. The region's 2,500 native plant species make the Sonoran Desert the world's lushest arid land; here you can find some

300 types of cacti, out of a world total of perhaps 1,600—including the saguaro, which, strange to say, is a cousin many times removed of spinach.

It was not always this dry and austere. Some 200 million years ago, the present region of the Sonoran Desert, then positioned alongside the Earth's equator in a location somewhere near the present south-central Pacific, lay under a giant inland sea bordered by swamplands. Into this sea were washed grains of river-borne and wind-borne sand that floated to the bottom, along with the bodies of fossil fish, insects, and arachnids—fossilized ancestral jellyfish, horseshoe crabs, and dragonflies figure prominently in exposed rock strata—to form chemically hardened layers of earth that eventually reached thicknesses of a mile and more. When the sea dried up, these layers of sandstone, limestone, and shale, no longer suppressed by water, rose and in turn were worn down by wind and water, molded into weird patterns by the Earth's forces, and sometimes reborn as isolated upthrusts of mineral-rich metamorphic rock.

At several points that followed over millions of years, the region underwent extensive volcanism that formed tall mountain peaks. The Tucson Mountains, in which the western part of Saguaro National Park stands, are the ancient, weathered results of this activity; the Rincon Mountains, at the park's eastern extreme, are

TOP: A saguaro forest marches toward the sheer walls of the Tucson Mountains. CHUCK LAWSEN

ABOVE: Burrowing owls are among the many animals that make their homes in saguaro trunks. C.K. LORENZ

newer and less weathered. As the mountains aged, they shed their loose rocks, which accumulated at their bases in great alluvial fans, or *bajadas*, and were carried off by rain and gravity into the valleys. Underlain by ancient impermeable clays and granite formations, these valleys, or grabens, filled to a depth of more than a mile, forming a gravelly bowl that eventually filled nearly to the surface with rainwater—an embarrassment of riches that helps account for the comparatively lush vegetation the Sonoran Desert enjoys today.

Some 50 million years ago, the still-temperate region burst forth with a new kind of tropical vegetation, the palm tree, then as now associated with the tropics. Another tropical plant was the ancestor of the saguaro, adapted to drink its fill in the rainy jungle. Over the following eons, as the region gradually began to dry, the palms retreated, leaving small relic populations of palm trees in the remote mountains of the lower Colorado River valley and central Arizona. (Most of the palm trees in cities such as Tucson and Phoenix were imported decades ago from California, which had brought them in from the tropics.) Ten thousand years ago, the Sonoran Desert

began to dry up definitively, taking on its present characteristics. Inland seas became playas, or sand beaches; narrow streams replaced broad rivers; and water-loving cacti such as the saguaro were left high and dry.

In time *Carnegeia gigantea* adapted to the new conditions, hoarding water—a mature adult can store nine tons—for use in times of drought. It also took to hugging to the rocky flanks of volcanic mountains. One reason the saguaro is so lush in Saguaro National Park is the warmth of the foothills in which the forests sit; at higher elevations, freezing temperatures are common in winter, but relatively rare down below, where meltwater assures the saguaros a steady supply of nourishment. Another reason is geological: The 1.5-billion-year-old fingers of diorite, a kind of volcanic rock, that stretch out from the mountains, are as hard as iron, but all those years have worn little fissures into the stone that saguaro roots have used to anchor themselves to the soil. "When you have a rocky substrate," says Tucson-based saguaro researcher Bill Peachey, "you don't have the rodents to eat the seeds that get down into the cracks. Mix that with warm temperatures

and rainfall, and you have most of the requirements for a healthy population of saguaros."

So, by any measure, the saguaro is an oddball of a plant. Although saguaros have been in this part of the world for eons, they don't really belong in the desert at all. Yet here they are, and Saguaro National Park stands as a fine testimonial to their importance to this place, environmental and cultural, as if to say, with the Tohono O'odham: These are our kin, and they deserve our protection.

Unlike many desert plants, but like humans, saguaros can live to a ripe old age. A 30-year-old cactus will be only a yard high, but when it hits the equivalent of adolescence, it begins to grow more quickly. By the time it has doubled its age it will have quintupled its height, and a few years later it will begin to sprout arms. A 40-foot-tall specimen may be anywhere from 150 to 200 years old, nearing the end of its lifespan, born before Anglos settled in the Southwest.

Unlike the Tohono O'odham, the first Europeans to arrive in the Sonoran Desert had little use for the saguaro. One of them, a Jesuit priest named Ignaz Pfefferkorn, wrote that "the plant is valuable only for its fine fruit, for otherwise, despite its size and thickness, it is a soft stuff, unfit for any conceivable use." Many of the newcomers who followed had much the same regard for the saguaro, and when ranchers came into Arizona in numbers in the 1880s, bringing in as many as 2 million head of cattle, the great forests began to disappear. Industrious creatures, cows eat whatever plants they happen upon, and saguaro pups—you'll find them under the harboring shelter of grass and mesquite, not far from their parents—were a favorite treat. Added to this, ranchers had a habit of killing the coyotes, wolves, and cougars they encountered, so that the rodent population exploded. Packrats and jackrabbits finished off whatever pups the cattle had overlooked, and soon, across the Sonoran Desert landscape, only mature saguaros stood.

The rise of large-scale agriculture made matters worse still. Beginning in the 1910s, farmers in

ABOVE: Saguaros, brittlebush, and chollas glow in sunset light. GEORGE H.H. HUEY
BOTTOM LEFT TO RIGHT (THIS PAGE AND OPPOSITE PAGE): Saguaro buds open into bright white flowers in late spring, heralding the arrival of heat. BRUCE GRIFFIN
A golden prickly pear flower beckons bats, insects, and other pollinators. GEORGE H.H. HUEY
A collared lizard soaks up rays on a warm rock in Saguaro National Park. C.K. LORENZ
A Gambel's quail, a familiar denizen of saguaro country, surveys his domain. G.C. KELLY

ABOVE: A stand of saguaros, thought to be humans by the desert's native peoples, admire a sunset over the Silver Bell Mountains. JACK DYKINGA

Arizona and Sonora, Mexico, were clearing huge tracts of land for cash crops like cotton and winter vegetables. Millions of saguaros were scraped from the soil. And not only that: One of the saguaro's main pollinators is the sphinx moth, which thrives in moist, irrigated fields. From those heavily fertilized farmlands it carried pesticides to the saguaro, which caused the fruit to die.

Multiple causes contributed to the same effect. In the 1930s the newly created Saguaro National Monument (later changed to Park status) was nationally promoted as the world's greatest "cactus forest," populated by tall, multiple-armed saguaros numbering in the millions. By 1985 much of that forest had disappeared. The intervening half-century had been punctuated by a quiet but steady scientific debate over who, or what, was to blame—and what to do about it. Few clear answers emerged.

One, however, was this: For several days in February 1939, Tucson lay in the grip of an uncommonly cold freeze, with daytime temperatures rising only to 25 degrees. In the months that followed, rangers at Saguaro National Monument noticed that more and more hitherto healthy cacti were dying, toppling over where they stood. On their corpses was found something that no ranger had seen before: pockets of brown ooze.

For the next two decades, local scientists joined rangers at the monument—which became Saguaro National Park in 1995—to conduct a battery of experiments aimed at defeating this strange new disease, now dubbed "brown rot." Following the model of livestock-disease specialists, they first tried removing infected "herds," leveling 320 acres of once-prime cactus forest with bulldozers and drag chains and burying the felled cacti, now doused with kerosene, in a mass grave. When the disease continued to spread, antibiotics were injected into and pesticides sprayed upon mature saguaros in the hope that if germs or insects were carriers of rot, one tactic or the other would take care of the offender.

Neither contained the epidemic, and by the mid-1950s the scientists gave up their search for a cure. Instead, University of Arizona professor of plant pathology Stanley M. Alcorn took over a monitoring program that had begun in 1940, tracking the progress of brown rot in cacti throughout the monument's east and west branches. Fellow scientists continued the program, and while they still haven't figured out what caused what they call the "great die-off," they do note that the plants at Saguaro National Park have been much healthier since. One cause, they venture, was the absence of cattle on the land after the area gained national-monument status.

With that, younger cacti had a chance of surviving. As plant scientist Tom Orum remarks, "Old plants seem to be more susceptible to rot, and if you don't have young ones to replace them, you don't have much hope of averting extinction."

Extinction has been averted. Look around, and you'll see that everywhere in Saguaro National Park, the cactus pups are thriving. Thanks to the good work of scientists, park rangers, and concerned citizens, the saguaro now seems safe from danger everywhere in its range except where cities such as Tucson, Phoenix, and Hermosillo are scraping the cacti away to grow even larger. This is the national park system at its very best: a place of safe harbor, of preservation, of study, a place where generations of the world's citizens can come to partake of the glory that is the American land. It is a comfort to know that *Carnegeia gigantea*, our kin in this vast and lovely desert, will endure for countless generations to come.

Location

On the eastern and western edges of Tucson, approximately 120 to 140 miles from Phoenix.

East District/Rincon Mountain District: From Interstate 10, take Exit 275 north to Escalante Road. Turn right, merge onto Old Spanish Trail, and follow the signs to the park. West District/Tucson Mountain District: From Interstate 10, take Exit 242 (Avra Valley Road) to Sandario Road, then turn left and follow the signs to the park.

Activities

Hiking, walking, bird-watching. Backcountry camping is permitted in the Saguaro Wilderness Area, located in the Rincon Mountain District. Check at the visitors centers for nature walks and other programs. Both visitors centers have shops offering food, drink, and other items. Elsewhere the park has no services, so carry water and snack food. Wear sturdy shoes for walking along the park trails. Please note that federal law prohibits collecting plants, rocks, and fossils, and feeding or transporting wildlife.

For more information

Saguaro National Park
3693 South Old Spanish Trail
Tucson, AZ 85730–5601
Rincon Mountain District: (520) 733-5153
Tucson Mountain District: (520) 733-5158
Headquarters: (520) 733-5100
www.nps.gov/sagu

ABOVE: Saguaro cacti drink up sunset light. JACK DYKINGA

Casa Grande Ruins National Monument

The ancient Hohokam people of the Sonoran Desert, according to the eminent archaeologist Emil W. Haury, came into what is now Arizona as a fully developed culture, perhaps having migrated north from Mesoamerica by way of the western Sierra Madre over a period of many years. They carried stories of that long journey, and they brought architectural traditions that point to southerly origins, such as ballcourts and pyramids. Among those traditions, it seems, was a talent for building tall mud buildings such as those of the desert nations of Oman and Yemen today, a talent so impressive that European newcomers to the Gila River Valley guessed that the four-story structure, which rose sometime before 1350, was built not by Aztecs but by the Egyptians themselves.

The Hohokam had been in the Gila valley for hundreds of years before Casa Grande rose to greet the sky. They were growing cotton near the site of present-day Phoenix at about A.D. 250, when many of their major cities, such as Snaketown, were founded, and they traded with the peoples of Mesoamerica, California, and even the Great Plains. Their canals sustained a vast population of some 60,000 at the peak of Hohokam civilization, and from those canals grew a political system that the desert had not seen before, one capable of erecting such great structures.

The mere presence of such a building suggests that Casa Grande was a place of importance—perhaps a commercial, administrative, or religious center. No one is certain, though stories told by the O'odham, descendants of the Hohokam, suggest that Casa Grande might have served all three purposes. Whatever the case, Casa Grande was abandoned in about 1450, a time of great upheaval throughout the Southwest. The people were, in the O'odham phrase, *huhugam*—"all gone"—leaving this mysterious, and most impressive, town as testimonial to their civilization.

For more information

Casa Grande Ruins National Monument
1100 W. Ruins Drive
Coolidge, AZ 85228
(520) 723-3172
www.nps.gov/cagr

BELOW: Casa Grande Ruins National Monument protects the remnants of an important Hohokam village built some 700 years ago. TOM DANIELSEN

Tumacácori National Historical Park

The Spanish conquest of Mexico, which began in the early 16th century, took only a few years. Settling the country, which included what is now Arizona, proved to be a generations-long process, during which Spanish soldiers and missionaries founded a system of forts and small churches that extended northward like spokes from Mexico City and Guadalajara. Their aim was to convert the indigenous peoples and make them citizens of the Spanish crown, thus eliminating the need to fund a large army to protect the northern frontier.

Founded by Jesuit explorer and missionary Francisco Eusebio Kino in 1691, the mission of San Cayetano de Tumacácori, now Tumacácori National Historical Park, was situated in a near-ideal location: Its dense forest of cottonwoods, willows, and sycamores provided both lumber and shade, while the fertile bottomland of the Santa Cruz River and the game-rich Santa Rita Mountains gave the mission a solid supply of food. Few of the churches and missions founded by Father Kino remain today, and fewer still in good shape. Tumacácori has been very well maintained over the years, and the site gives us a good idea of how the missions were established and operated.

Tumacácori is also the setting for a wonderful bit of Arizona folklore. In 1891, it seems that Judge William H. Barnes, chiefly known for his ability to make endless speeches on civic themes, received a late-night visit from a gaunt man in vestments who had a curious tale to tell. The man, who said he was a priest from Spain, produced a map that he claimed to have found in the vault of a church in his homeland. Etched with strange-sounding words that were quite familiar to the good judge—Tumacácori, San Xavier del Bac, Nogales—the map had led the supposed priest to the terra incognita of the Arizona Territory, where it promised to reveal the trail to a vast treasure.

The priest asked Judge Barnes to suggest the services of a few good churchgoing men to help him in his quest.

When he had assembled them, the priest led the company off to Tumacácori Mission, where one of the men produced a shovel and dug a hole at a certain distance from the ancient church's altar. The priest descended into a small hidden chamber, returning with several metal cases full of gold bullion. That was all he needed to feed the poor of his parish, he said, and he promised that if the men would help him bring his treasure to the Southern Pacific Railroad depot in Tucson, they could keep the rest of the loot for themselves.

The priest returned to Spain, bullion in tow, having left a small donation with his fellow priests at Saint Augustine Cathedral in downtown Tucson. A few days later, his eager assistants made their way back to Tumacácori, only to find that "either the landmarks had changed or they did not follow the directions of the chart closely." Judge Barnes, who now had the map, went there himself with no success. One of his friends later claimed to have found an old mine shaft by following its directions, but the veins seemed to have been played out years and years before.

The map, of course, has long since disappeared. And no good resident of Arizona has ever admitted to having taken part in the effort to uncover the treasure it promised to produce.

For more information

Tumacácori National Historical Park
1891 East Frontage Road
Tumacácori, AZ 85640
(520) 398-2341
www.nps.gov/tuma

TOP: Built at the site of a Tohono O'odham village, Tumacácori National Historical Park preserves a late colonial Spanish mission. TOM DANIELSEN

ABOVE: The Franciscan administrators of Tumacácori employed native builders to replicate European architectural forms, such as this arch. JACK DYKINGA

life in a
hard land

organ pipe cactus national monument

Flowering brittlebush
awaits a rainstorm over
the Ajo Mountains.
WILLARD CLAY

organ pipe cactus national monument

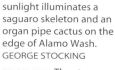

f you were to study a physical map of the world, following the tropics of Cancer and Capricorn 30 degrees on either side of the equator, you would see that, distributed with suspicious regularity, a brown band of drylands circles the planet. These, the deserts of the world, lie in the so-called horse latitudes, where constant high-pressure systems separate the westerlies and trade winds, driving away the rain clouds, swirling above the earth to the music of global temperature variations and the Coriolis effect produced by Earth's rotation in space. Many lie behind mountains, which cast great stone shadows that block air from wetter places. Deserts, which make up some 20 percent of the planet's surface, comprise harsh environments: landscapes of burning sands and desiccated vegetation, gravel and dead streambeds, and everywhere a chaos of stone and dust.

The word *desert* itself conjures up mystery, evoking the lonely emptiness of *Beau Geste* and *Flight of the Phoenix*—filmed, as it happens, among lofty sand dunes two hours' as-the-crow-flies drive from Organ Pipe Cactus National Monument, that desert place par excellence. That mystery may be a sign of its imprecision, for *desert* describes a wide range of landscapes. In fact, *desert* is so broadly defined that it is difficult to use the word precisely: the Sonoran Desert is dry, to be sure, but much less so than the central Sahara, which is the image most of us conjure up when the word reaches our ears or eyes.

Still, a few things in common distinguish deserts from other places: irregular and modest rainfall, the low level of moisture in the soil, the swift winds and correspondingly high evaporation rate of surface waters, poorly developed drainage systems, widely spaced plant life, and rocky or sandy ground.

The desert at Organ Pipe, where the comparatively lush Sonoran upland environment shades off into the hotter, drier, lower coastal plain of Sonora and the Colorado River delta, hosts those widely spaced plants of the definitive desert—the imposing organ pipe cactus, *Stenocereus thurberi*. It's a relative of the saguaro, cardon, night-blooming cereus, and the senita, with which the organ pipe cactus is often confused. The plant's closely packed branches look something like its namesake, the pipe organ of cathedral and nickelodeon renown. So thickly concentrated are those branches, in fact, that the organ pipe looks as if it has no center, no trunk; the oldest of these magnificent cacti can stand 25 feet tall and bear the weight of more than a hundred branches. Like the taller saguaro, *Stenocereus* takes a good while to attain any height; it is scarcely 6 inches tall at 10 years of age, scarcely 3 feet tall at 20, when, having survived all the dangers of childhood, it begins to grow more quickly, reaching its full growth at about 40. From there it goes on to live a long and generally healthy life, giving shelter and sustenance to doves, elf owls, cactus wrens,

OPPOSITE Late afternoon sunlight illuminates a saguaro skeleton and an organ pipe cactus on the edge of Alamo Wash. GEORGE STOCKING

BELOW LEFT: The stems of the organ pipe cactus seem custom-built to deter predators. DAVID W. LAZAROFF

BELOW RIGHT: Mexican goldpoppies surround the skeleton of a cholla cactus in the Puerto Blanco Mountains. JACK DYKINGA

kangaroo rats, bats, and other creatures and providing the delicious fruit that in Mexico is called *pitahaya*.

South of the border, in the warm coastal lands of Sonora, *Stenocereus* is quite common. In the United States, apart from a few mavericks, it is confined to this sprawling, 516-square-mile monument, where it lives among 25 other cactus species and a host of other plants and animals: 277 bird species, 70 kinds of mammals, 46 reptile species, 76 butterfly varieties and counting, and more. Not bad at all for a desert, a place whose Latin original, *desertus*, means "abandoned."

Absences of water, abundances of wind. It would seem a strange place, the desert, for humans to settle, but there have been people in this desert for millennia. For anyone who thrills at the clear air, brilliant mornings, and flaming sunsets of the desert, why they came is no mystery.

The native peoples of Organ Pipe had few luxuries. They dressed simply—and barely. They lived in low, well-ventilated huts, sometimes built partway underground and covered with branches and layers of earth. They knew what it meant to live in heat, aridity, and sometimes scarcity, which makes it all the more unfortunate that early European travelers to this area did not take the time out to interview them about their secrets. Instead, we have a history of misapprehension, one example of which is in the very name of the rugged mountains that tower over the eastern flank of the monument. Now, imagine a Spanish lancer galloping through clumps of *Stenocereus* and cholla, rounding a bend to find one of the Tohono O'odham (Desert People) or Hia-ced O'odham (Sand People) who made their homes here. The soldier may have asked, "*¿Donde estamos?*"—Where are we?—to which the O'odham may have said something like "*aw-aho.*" Hmmm, the soldier would have thought, Ajo, the place of garlic. And sure enough, he would have discovered, in time, that a native plant called the desert lily has that nose-tickling flavor so beloved in the cuisines of the Mediterranean. The O'odham's answer did not mean "garlic," though, but rather "the place where the paint comes from," for in the red rocks of the Ajo Mountains are abundant minerals that provided the O'odham with ceremonial makeup.

So, too, animals have much to tell us about the skills and adaptations required to live in places where heat is abundant and rainfall scarce. Consider the kangaroo rat, for instance, a familiar presence in Organ Pipe, and, unluckily for him, the favorite food

ABOVE: Teddy bear cholla and brittlebush line the rolling hills of the Ajo Plain. ROBERT G. MCDONALD

RIGHT: An organ pipe cactus flourishes among cholla, brittlebush, and poppies in the heart of the national monument dedicated to it. JACK DYKINGA

TOP LEFT: Late afternoon sunlight illuminates an organ pipe cactus among more numerous saguaros. GEORGE STOCKING

TOP RIGHT: Wild hyacinth flowers find a home on an accommodating organ pipe cactus. ROBERT G. MCDONALD

ABOVE: Lupine and mustard evening primrose flourish in the intermittently flowing Alamo Wash, on the eastern end of Organ Pipe Cactus National Monument. LARRY ULRICH

of the ringtail, a member of the raccoon family that also frequents this place. To top it off, the kangaroo rat is also a favorite snack for snakes.

Kangaroo rats like to make their homes in burrows tucked away among places in which it is easy to hide—the maze of branches of an organ pipe cactus, say. Those burrows are a marvel of engineering, and they repay the organ pipe and other obliging desert plants by distributing oxygen to tightly compacted desert soils, helping maintain a healthy layer of vegetation. They also wind up providing a roof for many other animals—wolf spiders, tarantulas, burrowing owls, salamanders, turtles, skunks, badgers, and other species that have adapted to the desert's heat by finding cool comfort underground. All of these creatures can be found in Organ Pipe Cactus National Monument, where they do quite well.

It also helps to keep your footprints small, as the ecologists might say—in other words, to make do with less. Consider *Stenocereus* itself, which, like all cacti, has evolved to maximize water conservation. It has no leaves by which water can be lost; it has an elaborate and extensive root system that seeks out water from far afield; it has developed a skin of manifold pleats, tissue that expands and contracts with the water available to it; it has developed a modest (as compared to, say, the cholla or hedgehog cactus) spiny armor to

discourage thirsty passersby from chomping down on it for a drink. Moreover, the organ pipe cactus, like its kin, can actually hold its breath—that is, seal off its pores during the hottest, driest, most water-robbing parts of the day, and then open them to release oxygen and take in a fresh store of carbon dioxide during the cooler hours of the night. That's a neat trick—as neat as the kangaroo rat's ability to conjure up water from the sun-dried seeds and fruits it gathers up and stows underground.

It also helps to have a certain learned fearlessness in the way of the nonchalant roadrunner, which lives in Organ Pipe in abundance. We know too little about this strange bird, and what Paolo Emilio Botta, an Italian acting as a scout for French investors in the Far West, wrote to his family in 1827 still hasn't been improved on: *Geococcyx californianus*, he noted, is "a running bird to which is attributed the ability to kill snakes for food. It has a long tail which it raises to an almost perpendicular position. It seldom flies but runs almost as fast as a horse." (Botta is remembered in the annals of science for discovering the ruins of the Mesopotamian city of Nineveh and the fabled palace of the Assyrian tyrant, Sargon, archaeological masterpieces.)

The O'odham knew the roadrunner much more intimately, and they assigned him the job of mapping out their territory. Roadrunner, *Tadai*, raced about this way and that, looking for the boundaries of earth and water and showing the people where to live—not least among the habitable places this lovely landscape of cactus and rock.

Understanding, adaptability, intelligence, survival: Organ Pipe is a place of demands, of exigencies, of extremes. It is also a place where one of the world's major ecosystems—that of the Sonoran Desert—endures almost unchanged, even as so much of the Sonoran Desert is changing so rapidly, reason for its having been designated an International Biosphere Reserve by the United Nations. Come and see, visiting the ever-instructive plants and animals of this desert haven—a fine classroom for anyone who would spend time in the dry country.

Location

Approximately 150 miles southwest of Phoenix. From Interstate 10, travel west to Exit 112, State Route 85, and follow it through Gila Bend, Ajo, and Why. The monument is 22 miles (35.4 km) south of Why. From Tucson (also approximately 150 miles distant), follow State Route 86 to Why, then turn south onto State Route 85.

Activities

Hiking, walking, bird-watching. Camping is permitted at the monument campground on a first-come, first-served basis; backcountry camping is also allowed with a permit. The visitors center offers slide shows, lectures, and other programs.

For more information

Organ Pipe Cactus National Monument
10 Organ Pipe Drive
Ajo, AZ 85321
(520) 387-6849
www.nps.gov/orpi

ABOVE: Evening primrose and woolly daisy are familiar flowers on the lower flanks of the Ajo Mountains. LARRY ULRICH

Ironwood Forest National Monument

Great columnar cacti such as the organ pipe and saguaro are characteristic of portions, but only portions, of the Sonoran Desert. A rather more wide-ranging character is the ironwood tree, *Olneya tesota*, which extends from deep into Mexico across Arizona and even into southeastern California. Ironwood is astonishingly sturdy, much heavier than mahogany and consequently difficult to cut, which has been much to the tree's advantage over the eons; about the only thing capable of felling an ironwood tree is mistletoe.

In recent times, however, chain saws have been brought into the equation, and vast forests of ironwood trees have suffered the consequences. Ironwood Forest National Monument, which is located about 25 miles northwest of Tucson and about 80 miles southwest of metropolitan Phoenix, preserves a great expanse of forest, one of the richest in the whole of the Sonoran Desert. Within its 129,000 acres also lie several desert mountain ranges, low but very rugged, and several sites of archaeological and historic interest, including Santa Ana del Chiquiburitac, the last of the Spanish colonial missions to be built in what is now Arizona.

Though it is a hot time of year, early summer sees *Olneya tesota* at its finest, when it puts forth spectacular dark purple and rose-red blossoms. At other times of year ironwood lives up to its redoubtable name, with its steely-gray bark and leaves. Whenever you visit, you will find yourself in a very special corner of the world.

For more information

Ironwood Forest National Monument
BLM Tucson Field Office
12661 East Broadway Blvd.
Tucson, AZ 85748–7208
(520) 258-7200
www.blm.gov/az/ironwood/ironwood.htm

ABOVE: Morning light streams across the saguaro and prickly pear cactus below Raggedtop Mountain, in Ironwood Forest National Monument. GEORGE STOCKING

BELOW: Ironwood blooms in front of saguaro cactus. BRUCE GRIFFIN

an island of stone

chiricahua national monument

Icicles form on a rocky wilderness at Chiricahua National
Monument during an autumn storm. RANDY PRENTICE

chiricahua national monument

t he smallest form a mountain can take is a
grain of sand.

Which is to say that stones have lives, as humans
do, if unfathomably eternal ones. Just as a law of
thermodynamics tells us that energy can be neither
created nor destroyed, so it is that stone is a constant of
the Earth on which we live, there at the beginning, there at the end.
But that constant presence is really an unending process of changes:
Lava spews up from below the world's surface, cools, and solidifies
in the form of igneous (that is, fire-born) rock. With the passage
of much time, this rock can be bent and warped like so much clay.
Water, too, usually in the form of ice, can break it down into tiny
flecks of sand, which will someday be compressed and turn into
stone, ready to be melted down into lava—and so the process begins
anew, an endless cycle of transformations until the end of time.

Mountains wear down to sand, the sand that crunches beneath
my feet on this quiet morning, standing before the sheer wall of
the Chiricahua Mountains of southeastern Arizona. Over the eons,
those sand playas, the Spanish word for "beaches," saw duty on
the floors of ancient oceans, which ebbed and receded. Above the
playas loomed great reefs of rock such as the Chiricahuas, the largest
single mountain chain in southern Arizona, born when massive fault
blocks pushed skyward while the separating valleys, our seafloors
metaphorical or real, dropped away. Because they resemble islands
in the sea and interact with the desert much as an island does with
the surrounding waters, naturalists call the pine-clad peaks of the
Sonoran Desert "sky islands." One bit of islandlike behavior is these
mountains' tendency to isolate plant and animal populations, giving
them slight variations from their kin on other mountains. Given my
experiences with them over the years, for instance, I can say with
some confidence that the black bears here are bolder than their
cousins in, say, Colorado or California. You have only to see one
or two of them ambling through your campsite, and I'd venture to
guess that you might come to the same conclusion.

A century ago, pondering how mountains related to the low
country surrounding them, the pioneering naturalist C. Hart
Merriam developed a concept he called "life zones." Merriam studied
the San Francisco Peaks north of Flagstaff and concluded that what
made Arizona special was its range of elevations, from near sea level
at Yuma to the 12,633-foot rise of Humphreys Peak. He arrived at a
formula whereby every thousand-foot climb in elevation corresponded
to the biological changes one would encounter by traveling 300 miles
north of the Mexican border. In Arizona, he counted six such life
zones: the Hudsonian, represented only by the highest peaks of the
San Francisco range, with their lichen-and-tundra associations that
echoed those of subarctic climes; the Canadian, marked by the vast

OPPOSITE: Punch and Judy, a named rock formation along the Heart of Rocks
Trail in Chiricahua National Monument, reaches skyward. LES DAVID MANEVITZ

TOP: Cochise Head looms over the labyrinth of stone along the Heart of
Rocks Trail. LARRY ULRICH

ABOVE: Chiricahua maple and Schott's yucca line the south fork of Cave Creek
Canyon, Chiricahua National Monument. PAUL GILL

coniferous forests of ponderosa pine, spruce, and Douglas fir of the high Mogollon Rim and the tops of mountain islands such as the Chiricahuas; the Transition zone, where stunted piñon and juniper replace the tall trees; the Upper Sonoran, with its mesquite forests and grasslands, beginning at about 6,500 feet, its characteristic saguaro forests that have come, for better or worse, to stand for the whole of Arizona in a thousand advertisements and Western movies; the Lower Sonoran, a zone of sunscorched sand and black volcanic rock; and the unlikely Tropical, attested to by a few inland oases and the lagoons of the lower Colorado River.

Merriam's scheme has been edited, altered, tinkered with in the years since, but the fact remains that the Chiricahuas, along with a few other tall ranges in southern Arizona, contain five of those six life zones, making them nearly worlds unto themselves, taking in a continent's worth of environments.

Let us go traveling. As we climb from their sandy base at a few hundred feet, passing across lands administered by the U.S. Forest Service before entering the national monument proper, we arrive in the foothills of the Chiricahuas, habitat for hundreds of animal and plant species. There the erosive force of water carves tree-lined canyons, often with small streams or springs tucked away inside, luring in myriad butterflies and moths, mammals like the javelina and the

ringtail, and a fantastic variety of bird life. The understory of streamside trees is just about the favorite place on Earth for a great many kinds of hummingbirds, who set the air abuzz with their frantic whirring as they dart from flower to flower—one reason, but only one, why birding enthusiasts from all over the world travel to the Chiricahuas in all seasons to add to their life lists.

We climb higher, ever upward through Bonita Canyon to Massai Point, at 6,870 feet the end of the Chiricahua National Monument scenic drive. Looking to the west, we see forests of rock spires, a great jumble of stone that the old-timers called "hoodoos" or "goblins," stretching down into the canyons below us. So tall and noticeable are these hoodoos that travelers on airliners passing above, in daylight, can easily pick them out.

The Apaches called this place "the land of standing rocks," and those old-timers dubbed it "a wonderland of rocks," both very good names for the vista that greets us. Here, deep within the mountains, visitors can see just about every kind of curious formation that Arizona has to offer, from spooky hoodoos to finger rocks, from boulder fields to rank after rank of spectacular spires and impossibly balanced rocks—and, as a bonus, the rare finds called spherulites, volcanic hailstones thrown up by ancient eruptions and then cooled in place into strange forms. The geologist Halka Chronic refers to this place as

TOP LEFT: A half moon rises between the volcanic rhyolite spires of Echo Canyon. RANDY PRENTICE

TOP RIGHT: A ringtail, cousin to the raccoon, scales a tree in Chiricahua National Monument. G.C. KELLY

ABOVE: The Chiricahua Mountains are a paradise for birds such as this black-chinned hummingbird, and for birders as well. G.C. KELLY

the product of "a wild orgy of volcanic eruptions 30 to 25 million years ago," and the Chiricahuas saw plenty of wild action, a single event of which, the Turkey Creek Caldera eruption, is estimated to have been a thousand times more powerful than the 1980 eruption that tore apart Mount St. Helens.

Sand and rock, ash and pumice make for a devilish playground. Throw these ingredients into a fiery brew, and you have concoctions such as rhyolitic tuff, a rock that is paradoxically both hard and soft. Forming great columns, the tuff is here eroded, there protected by a hard caprock that keeps the softer material beneath it from entirely eroding away, teetering crazily; some of them stand as upright as soldiers on guard. The effect can be a little unnerving, just the kind of thing for a ghost story such as the Chiricahua Apaches, the proud inhabitants of this land, were fond of telling.

Long ago, a Chiricahua story goes, a beautiful maiden who always dressed in shimmering white deerskin went to a spring high in the mountains to fetch water. Her people waited and waited for her return, but she did not come back to their camp. They went to the spring and found her water jug, and then her tracks going even higher up into the mountains. They followed her as far as they could, but then her tracks went straight up the stone face of the summit and disappeared.

Her people called for the shaman to search out her lost spirit. He pondered and sang for four days, and then he announced, "She is still alive up there in the mountains." So the people went up to the stone face and sang until, finally, the cliff opened onto a hall full of wolves, bears, and mountain lions. The shaman sang some more, and as the people and animals joined in the song, another door opened, and there stood the maiden with a bear.

"Come with us," the shaman said. But the maiden refused, saying, "Stay close to this holy place; keep your camp near these mountains. I will always be among you, and no enemy will trouble you. Always keep this place within your sight." The people returned to their camp, but they decided to leave the mountains to hunt for food, and four days later they were massacred—by whom, the story does not say. And so it is that at night the animals cry in the mountains, calling for the people to return.

It's not a happy story, not by a long shot, but the Chiricahuas have a history that is as difficult as the land itself. The tutelary spirit of this place is a great Chiricahua Apache leader, and his story is tangled in accident and misfortune. It begins early on a cold winter morning in 1861, when a young man then known as Felix Ward, just barely a teenager, stole out of a ranch house in the Sonoita Valley a couple of ranges to the west and made his way toward the

Chiricahuas. Born to Mexican parents, he had few friends among his white neighbors, and his Irish stepfather and he were not getting along, so it seems reasonable to guess that he was looking for a happier life in the wild country.

The stepfather complained to the commander of a garrison of soldiers stationed nearby that Chiricahua Apaches had stolen the boy and some of his cattle. The Apaches, he added, rode with the war leader they called Cheis, "Oak Tree," in honor of his strength and endurance.

Sixty soldiers traveled to a Butterfield stagecoach camp below the Chiricahuas, the place where Fort Bowie National Historic Site now stands. There they found the man the whites called Cochise, who came down to pay his respects, bringing his wife, two of his children, and his brother along for the occasion. The lieutenant in charge invited them into his tent, then accused him of stealing John Ward's son and cattle. Cochise protested his innocence, but the officer, George Bascom, replied that he would hold Cochise's relatives prisoner until the boy was delivered. At that, contemporary reports tell us, Cochise sprang up, produced a hidden knife, slashed through the tent, and fled. He quickly reached the surrounding hills, still clutching the cup of coffee that the officer had served him, and waited,

ABOVE: Big tooth maple leaves line a streambed in the Chiricahua Mountains.
JACK DYKINGA

ABOVE: Sunset light lends rosy hues to the gray spires along Echo Park Trail. GEORGE STOCKING

RIGHT: The Wonderland of Rocks and Sugarloaf Mountain rise behind Inspiration Point, high in the Chiricahua Mountains. RANDY PRENTICE

occasionally appearing just out of range to call for the release of his family.

So it went for two weeks. Then, tired of waiting, Cochise and a hundred warriors appeared at the Butterfield stage station, chased away the soldiers' mules, and fired a few shots. The soldiers returned fire, killing a Butterfield employee, and then hunkered down while awaiting reinforcements. A superior officer arrived with 70 more soldiers, angry that Bascom had allowed Cochise to escape and that his warriors had taken hostages themselves, one of whom Cochise ordered to write a note to Bascom. "Treat my people well," it read, "and I will do the same by yours."

Instead, the Apaches killed their hostages, and the soldiers responded by hanging Cochise's brother and two of his brother's sons. Bascom released Cochise's wife and sons, however, and then took time to write an official report on what would come to be called the "Bascom Affair," in which he claimed that he had released Cochise on his own recognizance after the great chief promised that he would return Felix Ward to his family. The report had the desired effect: Cochise's name became widely known, synonymous with treachery, while Bascom received a promotion to captain.

Cochise was famous among his people, though few outsiders had seen him up close. Now, with his family's blood to avenge, he became a force of nature, and he swore to drive all foreigners from the Apache homelands. Just as the land itself was a sheltering island, the Chiricahuas lived apart from other people, isolated, traversing the sandy seas in terrible vengeance.

The war that followed lasted for 10 years. Finally, everyone tired of fighting, and peace talks began. A U.S. government agent, Tom Jeffords, an Arizona settler who had learned something of the Apache language and had evident respect for the culture, met with Cochise several times, hoping to convince the war leader to give up his fight before more died on either side. Cochise was willing to listen, but he had heard promises before, not least when an American general promised that he would make the Chiricahua Mountains the heart of a planned reservation for them. When it became clear that the general had no intention of doing so, Cochise continued the fight, even though he was quite ill for much of that time, and nearing 70 years of age.

Cochise died on June 8, 1874. His warriors took his body deep into the Dragoon Mountains, to the west of the Chiricahuas, lowered it into a crevice far from prying eyes, and rode their horses back and forth to destroy the trail leading up to the site. They then mourned their fallen leader for four days, sending up a cry of lamentation that spread across the broad desert valleys and echoed along the mountains. "The howl that went up from these people was fearful to listen to," said Jeffords, who knew of the location of the grave but never revealed it, though he was often pressured to do so. "They were scattered around in the nooks and ravines in parties, and as the howling from one rancheria would lag, it would be renewed with vigor in another."

The earth holds Cochise now, but he is remembered today, even as his spirit—or so some say—roams the Chiricahua Mountains. And as for young Felix Ward? Soon after leaving home, he was taken in by an Apache family. When he was 25, calling himself Mickey Free, he enlisted in the Apache scouts attached to the U.S. Army and soon was at work fighting the Chiricahuas. That war would last a decade beyond Cochise's death, with one of his lieutenants, a man named Goyahkla, leading the Chiricahuas in battle. He is better known to history by the name his Mexican enemies gave him: Geronimo.

The Chiricahua Apache people never did get their reservation, and they no longer exist as a distinct group. Their homeland baffled many of the white settlers who attempted to make their homes there. When they planted crops in the foothills, rabbits and bears and every kind of bird imaginable helped themselves, and so the farmers went on to greener pastures, leaving the mountains to ranchers, foresters, and the occasional prospector. Those who came found that they had to rely on their own resources; Faraway Ranch, a pioneer homestead within

Chiricahua National Monument, is testimonial to the hard work and perseverance of Swedish immigrants Neil and Emma Erickson, who made a little paradise for their family under conditions that most moderns would find hard to fathom.

Geologists and biologists from all over the country came there, too, to study the unusually diverse mountain range, a portion of which was set aside as Chiricahua National Monument in 1924. They had much to study. For the geologists, there was the deep past, of course, but also the future to consider, for the mountains continue to grow, even as the valleys below them sink ever so gradually, pressed down by the weight of the rocks the Chiricahuas shed. The mountains are also a prime example of "basin and range" topography, which describes the system of mountain islands that stretches from northern Mexico to southern Idaho, and that has no real counterpart anywhere else on Earth.

As for the biologists, they found in the Chiricahuas a natural laboratory where animals of the desert, mountains, and even Central American jungles met: hundreds of bird species, dozens of mammals, some of them creatures that were rarely seen and were even thought extinct or nearly so, such as short-tailed hawks, thickbill parrots, and, lately, jaguars. The Chiricahuas harbor the southernmost aspen groves in the United States, growing high among the ponderosa pines and Engelmann spruce trees of the topmost elevations. Rucker Canyon, in particular, in the mountains south of the national monument, is a place where fans of the quaking aspen go to mark the changing seasons.

Southern Arizona doesn't get much prettier than the Chiricahuas, and in few places on the planet are the forces of geology on such extravagant display. I return there as often as I can, which is never as often as I'd like, to watch the changing trees and the dramatic skies, hoping to catch a glimpse of Cochise's shade among the weirdly shaped rocks. Apart from the hyperactive black bears, ever-present snakes, and abundant birds, I often feel as if I have the monument's 12,000 acres to myself, isolated within isolation itself. That is just as it should be in this wilderness of stone, an island on the land.

Location

Approximately 240 miles southeast of Phoenix. From Phoenix, take Interstate 10 east to Exit 336 at Willcox, then follow State Route 186 for 36 miles southeast to the monument entrance.

Activities

Hiking, walking, camping, bird-watching. Check at the visitors center for nature walks and other programs.

For more information

Chiricahua National Monument
12856 East Rhyolite Creek Road
Willcox, AZ 85643
(520) 824-3560
www.nps.gov/chir

ABOVE: Historic Faraway Ranch, built by Swedish immigrants Neil and Emma Erickson more than 100 years ago, stands near the entrance to Chiricahua National Monument. GEORGE H.H. HUEY

Coronado National Memorial

Francisco Vasquez de Coronado, the governor of the province of Nueva Galicia, had a desire to see the distant frontiers of Spain's desert empire. Like so many of his compatriots, he also yearned for wealth, and when he heard tales of cities of gold, he assembled an army of 300 Spanish soldiers and more than 1,000 Indian porters. In February 1540, the army marched northward, making its way to the headwaters of the San Pedro River and crossing into what is now Arizona on the site of the Coronado National Memorial in mid-spring. Scholars argue over his route, but from reports from the Coronado expedition, we can guess that he proceeded northward across the Mogollon Rim to Zuni Pueblo, then ever onward.

They found no gold, not even at Zuni, which is thought to be the golden Cibola of legend; Coronado called it "a small rocky pueblo, all crumpled up, there being many farm settlements in New Spain that look better from afar." After taking a bad fall from his horse in northeastern Kansas, Coronado turned his men—now a mere handful, thanks to war and the rigors of the trek—southwestward and plodded back to Mexico.

The quest for gold ruined Coronado, as it would so many other conquistadores. A startled contemporary wrote to the Spanish emperor: "Francisco Vasquez came to his home, and he is more able to be governed in it than to govern outside it. He is lacking in many of his former fine qualities and he is not the same man he was when your Majesty appointed him to governorship." He retained his post as governor of Nueva Galicia for only another two years as his health steadily declined. Francisco Vasquez de Coronado died on his ranch outside Mexico City on September 22, 1554, at the age of 44. Nearly 400 years later, in 1952, President Harry S. Truman dedicated the monument in his honor.

For more information

Coronado National Memorial
4101 East Montezuma Canyon Road
Hereford, AZ 85615
(520) 366-5515
www.nps.gov/coro

ABOVE: Montezuma Pass, in Coronado National Memorial, commands a sweeping view of Mexico. GEORGE H.H. HUEY

index